Super-
structures

Experimental
Jetset

Published by Roma Publications
ISBN 978-94-92811-86-8

Roma 400
First edition: 2021

Graphic design: Experimental Jetset
Printing: Drukkerij Tienkamp, Groningen
Binding: Stronkhorst, Groningen
Distribution: Idea Books, Amsterdam
Proofreading: Dutton R. Hauhart

Annotated by Vasyl Cherepanyn, Leontine Coelewij, Linda van Deursen, Experimental Jetset, Owen Hatherley, Brad Haylock, Dirk van den Heuvel, Lieven Lahaye, Samata Masato, Tom McDonough, Kateryna Mishchenko, Other Forms, Mark Owens, Megan Patty, Adam Pendleton, Simon Reynolds, Ian F. Svenonius, McKenzie Wark, Lori Waxman, Mimi Zeiger

Super-
structures

Experimental
Jetset

Other publications by Experimental Jetset include *World of Money* (1998), *Words/Objects/People* (1998), *Advanced Economics* (1998), *Lost Formats Preservation Society* (Emigre, 2000), *Kelly 1:1* (Casco, 2002), *Two or Three Things I Know About Provo* (Moravian Gallery, 2012), *Automatically Arranged Alphabets* (Roma, 2015), *Statement and Counter-Statement: Notes on Experimental Jetset / Volume 1* (Roma, 2015/2017), *Interne Correspondentie 1* (Roma, 2018), *Interne Correspondentie 2* (Roma, 2019), *Full Scale False Scale: Notes on Experimental Jetset / Volume 3* (Roma, 2019)

Super-structures

Roma

Experimental Jetset

In the city,
there's a thousand things
I want to say to you

– The Jam, *In the City* (1977)

Chapters

Chapter 1

Super-structures Infra-structures Sub-structures Counter-structures[1] De-structures De-con-structures Con-structures Re-con-structures Macro-structures Micro-structures Ultra-structures Hyper-structures Anti-structures[2]

and other structures

Introduction

The city as an infrastructure for language / Language as an infrastructure for the city[3]

> *The city is a discourse,[4,5] and this discourse is actually a language: the city speaks to its inhabitants, as we speak to our city...*
>
> – Roland Barthes, "Semiology and Urbanism" (1967)

If the notion of modernism should ever be encapsulated in just one sentence, a good contender would be that famous line by Marx and Engels: "If humans are made by their environment, this environment has to be made human."[6] If there is one common denominator that seems to connect that wide range of disparate views and conflicting movements otherwise known as "modernism," it surely is the acute awareness[7] that we are shaped by our surroundings, coupled with a deep desire[8] to shape those surroundings ourselves.[9]

Following that line of thinking, it makes sense to interpret the city as the ultimate platform of modernism – the metropolis as the quintessential human-made environment, a forest made of walls and words.[10,11,12] And, needless to say, the notion of the city as an extension of language plays an important part within this concept of urban modernity. After all, what better way to create a human environment than to create a linguistic environment? Language lives inside us[13] – so our most modernist urge might be to try to reverse this situation, by living inside language. To speak with Heidegger:[14] "poetically, man dwells."[15] Our cities are poems, our words are buildings.[16,17]

Experimental Jetset, March 2018

1. The Constructivist City

Paper Architecture
Scale-model Socialism
Maquette Modularity
Bauhaus Bolshevism
Flatland Futurism
Utopian Geometry

1.1

Modernism is often described as a monolithic, singular entity – in our view, it is far from that. Modernism is a multitude of languages, dialects, and accents – a maelstrom[18] of opposing, clashing voices.[19] Manifestos, movements, tendencies, schools, groups, and splinter groups. Fictions, factions, fractions, and fragments. It's a storm blowing, spiralling us forward, propelling us right through history – from the invention of the printing press up until now. ("This storm is what we call progress.")

Within this messy modernist continuum, the beginning of the 20th century occupies an iconic position. From the rubble of violent wars, intense revolutions, grave disasters, and times of deep crises, small groups of artists and designers somehow managed to develop new aesthetic languages, trying to envision (with equal parts optimism and pessimism)[20] possible ways out of the ruins.[21]

Among these groups, we find the Constructivists: a loose subculture of artists, designers, and writers, mainly working in the Soviet Union (and other parts of Eastern Europe), roughly between 1917 and 1927 – in other words, during that unique, utopian moment between the Russian Revolution and the rise of Stalin. Names often associated with Constructivism are Kazimir Malevich, Alexander Rodchenko, El Lissitzky, Lyubov Popova, Vladimir Mayakovsky, and Vladimir Tatlin – but this list merely scratches the surface.[22]

In the same way that Constructivism[23] was one of the many movements within the maelstrom of modernism, the whole notion of Constructivism itself was a whirlpool of contrasting ideas and positions. Several groups, sub-groups, academies, institutes, journals, and individuals were in constant dialogue with each other, in a passionate struggle for utopia. Productivism, Suprematism, Cubo-Futurism, Cosmism, LEF, Agit-Prop, Prolet-Kult, Zaum, OBMOKhU, INKhUK, VKhUTEMAS, UNOVIS – the biotope of Constructivism reads as an ongoing, magical spell of mystical "-isms," occult abbreviations, and esoteric acronyms.[24,25,26]

Added to this, Constructivism also overlapped and connected (through initiatives such as the Constructivist International) with movements and schools such as Dada, Futurism, De Stijl, and Bauhaus – expanding the scope of Constructivism even further.

1.2

The city[27] is the ultimate modernist platform – it's not surprising therefore that Constructivism had a vested interest in the urban environment.[28] As the poet and playwright Vladimir Mayakovsky declared in 1917: "the streets are our brushes, the squares our palettes." Within the Constructivist imagination, the city became a language machine, a spatial poem,[29] a constant source of graphic agitation and propaganda. Through a system of para-architectural structures (newspaper kiosks, typographic pavilions, pop-activist billboards, speaker's tribunes), the city was turned into a three-dimensional manifesto – language as a place to dwell in.[30]

The Section for Artistic Labor (the revolutionary Soviet committee responsible for inviting artists and designers to develop these new forms of street furniture) was actually headed by a poet rather than an architect, which might explain the strong focus on typography within these projects.

But even the more massive architectural proposals (such as Vladimir Tatlin's's titanic *Monument to the Third International*,1919–1920) were treated as platforms to distribute language – after all, Tatlin's tower was meant as a gigantic radio transmitter, the giant spiralling structure designed to broadcast live speeches, straight from the Comintern.

Even factories were reimagined as devices for communication – in this regard, we should mention composer Arseny Avraamov's *Symphony of Factory Sirens* (1922), a musical performance that included actual industrial sirens and smoking chimneys.[31,32]

1.3
Most of these para-architectural structures remained unbuilt – like the October Revolution itself, the scale models, drawings, and collages never fulfilled their utopian potential. Tatlin's tower, a true icon of Constructivism, was never erected – although the existing scale model can be regarded as an impressive piece of para-architecture in itself.[33] Looking at historical photos of this oversized maquette[34] being paraded through Leningrad, one feels the borders (between technical drawing, scale model, street furniture, para-architecture, and actual architecture) simply melting into thin air. Models turn into buildings, buildings into models[35] – reality becomes a graphic collage, a manifesto of dreams unfulfilled[36] (or at least, not-yet-fulfilled).

Having said that, it might be wrong to regard these unbuilt structures as "unrealized."[37] As the Australian academic Maria Gough suggested (in a recent essay on Gustav Klutsis's fantastic *Screen/Tribune/Radio/Orator/Kiosk* drawings), a case can be made that these para-architectural proposals were indeed realized – through the printing press. By being circulated through books and magazines, these sketches and collages gained a material dimension that can easily rival that of actual architecture.[38]

As the Constructivists tried to realize their graphic language in the city, ultimately, it was the city that manifested itself in the graphic language of Constructivism.

2. The Situationist City

Subversive Cartography
Diagrammatic Nihilism
Proto-psychogeographies
Bitter topo/typologies
Monochromic Schematics
Disinfographics
Labyrinthic Urbanism

2.1

Out of the ashes of the great movements of the early 20th century (Bauhaus, Dada, Surrealism), a new generation of painters and poets emerged. Embittered by World War II, and highly critical of past avant-gardes, this new breed of modernists pushed an agenda that was meaner, leaner, and far more aggressive than previous efforts. In France, a theoretical street gang called the Lettrists splintered in two factions, one headed by the poet Isidore Isou, another centered on the filmmaker Guy Debord. In Denmark, the CoBrA-affiliated painter Asger Jorn founded the International Movement for an Imaginist Bauhaus (MIBI). And back in Amsterdam, another CoBrA member, artist Constant Nieuwenhuijs, turned his attention to architecture and urbanism – an interest that would lead to his long-running *New Babylon*[39] project (1956–1974).

When these groups eventually ran into each other (during a tumultuous conference in Alba, in the summer of 1956), the resulting collective named itself the Situationist International (SI).

Through a strategic process of purges, expulsions and exclusions,[40] the leadership of this platform fell more and more into the hands of Guy Debord, who streamlined the SI into an ultra-political, ultra-theoretical fighting unit. Militantly iconoclastic, the movement dedicated itself to Marxist-inspired attacks on the "Society of the Spectacle" (a model of current society in which everything is reduced to mere forms of representation). It seems only fitting that the twelve issues of the movement's journal (published between 1958 and 1969) came wrapped in minimalist metallic covers – each issue polished like an individual bullet.

2.2

Within the Situationist mindset, the city was meant to be treated as language – through a daily routine of aimless drifting (a method described as the *dérive*), the urban environment was to be read, analyzed (and criticized) as a text,[41,42] as a piece of prose or poetry. Roland Barthes (in "Semiology and Urbanism," 1967) and Michel de Certeau (in *The Practice of Everyday Life*, 1980) both characterized the specific relationship between the city and the wanderer as a dialogue,[43] a discourse, or a form of speech. It was the Situationists who explored this territory before them.

This notion, of the city as a text to be (close-)read,[44] is most clearly illustrated in the memorable paragraph from Michèle Bernstein's Situationist novel *All The King's Horses* (1960), in which a young girl asks one of the main characters what he studies. "Reification," he answers. The girl then assumes he must be working "with big books, and a huge table cluttered with papers" – to which the Debordian protagonist replies: "No, I walk... I mostly walk."[45] The implication is clear – streets are meant to be read, and to drift is to study.[46,47,48,49,50]

Since the city was seen as the main text, it also meant it could be annotated. And thus, the streets were inscribed with footnotes – in the form of graffitied slogans, subversive posters, and political pamphlets. Already in 1953, Debord famously painted *Ne Travaillez Jamais* on a wall near the Rue de Seine – and in that same year, Dutch photographer Ed van der Elsken took pictures of Lettrists in the streets of Paris, their baggy clothes filled with Proto-Punk slogans.

This apparatus of spatial footnotes grew to new heights during the student riots of 1968, when Paris was completely filled with Situationist-inspired slogans, political graffiti, typographic posters, and billboards turned into barricades. In the French journal *Utopie* (1967–1978), Jean Baudrillard described this brief moment (of "applied situationism") as follows:

> *Walls and words,*[51] *screen-printed posters and hand-made flyers, were the true revolutionary media in May 1968. The streets where speech started and was exchanged: everything that is an immediate inscription, given and exchanged. Speech and response, moving in the same time and in the same place, reciprocal and antagonistic.*

2.3

While the graphic language of the Situationists manifested itself in the city, the notion of the city simultaneously appeared in the graphic language of the Situationists – in the form of cartographic maps, diagrams, and collages. Guy Debord and Asger Jorn shared a fascination for the schematic language of subway maps and street plans – a language that perfectly lent itself for *détournement*, that typical Situationist method of visual appropriation.[52]

An iconic example of the Situationist use of diagrams[53] can be found in Debord's *The Naked City* (1957), a psychogeographic, cut-up, fold-out map of Paris.[54,55] This fragmented, subjective piece of cartography criticized the very notion of objective representation, while hinting at new ways to experience our material environment – a perfect illustration of the subversive relationship between printed matter and the city.[56,57]

3. The Provotarian City

Poetic Sloganeering
Open Language Machines
Blown-up Information Networks
Mass-Media Magick

3.1

In short, Provo was an Amsterdam anarchist movement that existed for just two years (1965–1967),[58] although its existence resonated for years to come, in the Netherlands and abroad.[59]

Through printed matter, conceptual activism, and speculative political proposals[60] (the *White Plans*), the Provo movement forever shaped the modernist landscape. Part art movement and part political party, Provo was a loose-knit collective consisting of individuals with very different ambitions: subversive agendas, artistic motives, utopian ideas, concrete plans. Between 1965 and 1967, these motives and agendas briefly overlapped, creating a unique and singular movement. A movement that liquidated itself in 1967, during a self-declared act of "auto-provocation."[61,62]

Right after the liquidation of Provo, some of the main founders remained active in various post-Provo groups. One of these activists was Rob Stolk (1946–2001), who played an important role in the early Dutch squatters' scene (Woningburo De Kraker, 1968),[63] in Aktiegroep Nieuwmarkt[64,65] (the action committee that successfully protested against the demolition of the Amsterdam Nieuwmarkt district, 1967–1976), and in the Maagdenhuisbezetting (the student occupation of the University of Amsterdam, 1969).

Already during the Provo years, Stolk's activism forced him to become a printer – since mainstream printers refused to handle the subversive (and sometimes illegal) Provo material, Stolk had no other option than to print these publications himself. And it was exactly Stolk's conceptual use of the printing press that played a crucial role in the relationship between Provo and the city.

3.2
At the heart of Provo is the triangle between the city, the movement, and the printing press.

Magazines were distributed in the streets,[66] posters were pasted to the walls, performances ("happenings") took place on public squares and around specific statues,[67] mystical slogans were being chanted (such as a repeated mantra of "ugh, ugh, ugh"), and pamphlets[68] were handed out to unsuspecting bystanders. Protesters filled the roads with smoke signals[69] (according to Dutch beat writer Jan Wolkers, "one of the oldest languages in the world"), while empty banners and white bikes[70] were being carried around during ludic marches. Through these graphic gestures and poetic spells, the city turned into a magick center for applied utopianism.[71]

Meanwhile, the (illegal) printing press of Provo had to be constantly moved, from one location to another, because there was always the danger of confiscation. In that sense, the printing press itself was on a constant *dérive* through the city, echoing the way the Provos themselves were drifting through the streets of Amsterdam – a perfect illustration of the symbiotic relationship between the city and the printing press.[72]

In the case of Provo, it can even be argued that the city itself became a printing press. Through graphic and poetic strategies, Provo turned the city into a place where ideas were enlarged, multiplied, and reproduced.[73] In other words, through Provo, the city revealed itself as a device for reproducing ideas – a metaphorical printing press.

3.3
It seems only natural that Provo (a movement so dedicated to the exploration of the city as a platform for graphic signs) used, as their main signature, a graphic sign representing the city.

The symbol of the apple,[74] also known as the "gnot sign," was conceived around 1962 by pre-Provo pioneers Bart Huges and Robert Jasper Grootveld, when they were looking for a sign to symbolize the notion of Amsterdam as the "Magies Sentrum"[75,76,77] ("Magick Center") of the world. Initially, the mark encapsulated a whole range of possible meanings: from a third eye to a fetus, from a skull to a butthole. In 1965, when the sign was adopted by the Provo movement, its meaning was narrowed down to the idea of the apple as a rendering of Amsterdam – an abstract map of the city, in which the circular outline represents the canals, the short stem (or stalk) symbolizes the Amstel river, and the dot depicts the Spui (the Amsterdam square where most of the Provo-related happenings took place). From then on, the gnot sign became the unofficial logo of the Provo movement, appearing frequently in print and on walls. In a sense, it is the perfect mark for Provo: a psychogeographical micro-map, grounding the Provo movement firmly in the material surroundings of Amsterdam.

Another architectural motif within the language of Provo is the brick wall pattern.[78,79] A clear example can be seen in the first few issues of the *Provo* journal, which came wrapped in brick-patterned covers (the handwritten word "Provo" appearing as graffiti on a wall). By turning printed matter into walls, walls were turned into printed matter – both equally valid as platforms for language.

4. The Post-Punk City

Dystopian Ambivalence
Fictional Corporations
Lost Formats
Ballardian Anarchitecture
Dark Modernism

4.1

When it comes to dating the exact period in which Punk took place, there are two possible approaches.
There is the long view: Punk as a continuous condition, an ongoing mentality – a narrative without ending ("Punk's Not Dead," and will never die), with roots stretching far back in history (Jon Savage, in his *Punk Etymology*, traces the word back to 1946, while Greil Marcus, in *Lipstick Traces*, reconnects Punk to the esoteric protestant sects[80] of the 16th century).
Next to that, there's the "big bang" model: Punk as a short, sharp shock[81] – a movement that only lasted for a few weeks (or perhaps even just a few days, or hours, or seconds) during that sweltering English heatwave of 1977 (the so-called "Summer of Hate"), transforming everything that took place afterwards into "Post-" (and everything that happened beforehand into "Proto-").

Surely, there's truth in both models.[82] Punk might have been a singular instant, linked to a very specific space/time axis – but obviously, it left traces in everything that happened afterwards, its echoes traveling far beyond 1977, and far beyond the English-speaking world.

In many ways, Punk can be seen as a scale model of modernism[83,84] itself – an arena of both constructive and destructive forces. Punk covers the full spectrum, from the applied utopianism of "Do-It-Yourself" to the dystopian nihilism of "No Future" – and everything in-between. This spectrum widens even further in the case of Post-Punk, when the original Punk Rock movement explodes and splinters into dozens of sub-sub-sub-cultures.[85] Synth-Pop, Two-Tone Ska, Mod Revivalism, Psychobilly, New Romanticism, No Wave, Noise Industrialism, Oi Workerism, American Hardcore[86] – the list goes on and on.

4.2
This pluralism within Punk[87] (and certainly within Post-Punk) might explain why it's near impossible to single out one specific way in which the graphic language of Punk manifested itself in the city.

Of course, one could always point to graffiti[88] – that great unifier and equalizer, connecting all movements and subcultures, from antiquity to the present.

Another link between Punk and the city[89] might be the specific, architectural way in which fashion was utilized by punks. Through the use of badges, patches, spikes, and studs, clothes were transformed into kiosk-like, para-architectural structures.[90] (In his essay "New Brutalists / New Romantics,"[91] Mark Owens does a brilliant job mapping out the similarities between Post-Punk textures and Brutalist surfaces).

4.3
For now, we'd like to focus on the notion of the "Ballardian," to provide yet another possible link between Post-Punk aesthetics and the urban environment. As many critics (such as Simon Reynolds, in *Rip it Up and Start Again*) have already pointed out, much Post-Punk imagery can be traced back to dystopian themes

originally developed by British sci-fi writer J.G. Ballard (1930–2009). High-rise alienation, subway armies, highway wastelands, concrete jungles – these motifs play an important role in both the graphics and lyrics of Synth-Pop, Two-Tone, and New Wave bands alike.

Most importantly, what Post-Punk shares with Ballard is a sense of "critical ambivalence."[92] Despite his dystopian visions, Ballard actually loved modernity – his attitude towards modern architecture was one of morbid fascination,[93] both affirmative and skeptical at the same time. The same sense of ambiguity can be found in the Post-Punk attitude towards corporate culture. Avoiding the traditional rock formats,[94] many Post-Punk bands remodeled themselves as corporations, organizations, industrial operations (think of groups like Public Image Ltd, Sigue Sigue Sputnik, Heaven 17, and Throbbing Gristle).[95] In an attempt to beat capitalism at its own game, these bands appropriated boardroom strategies, simultaneously embracing and attacking corporate culture.

From a modernist perspective, this "corporate turn"[96,97,98,99] seems perfectly in tune with that famous line from the original *Dada Manifesto* (1918): "To be a Dadaist means being a businessman or a politician, rather than an artist." Or, as Public Image Ltd would proclaim, some 65 years later (in the ambivalently titled "This Is Not a Love Song," 1983): "Big business is very wise / I'm crossing over into free enterprise."

The sleeve of PiL's *Live in Tokyo* (1983) seems to perfectly encapsulate this urgent sense of ambiguity. John Lydon is photographed against a spectacular, Pop-Art-like Tokyo backdrop, the PiL logo on his T-shirt flawlessly blending in with the brightly colored neon signs on the Shibuya buildings; the graphic language of Post-Punk, brutally inserting itself into the corporate cityscape – and vice versa.

Footnotes written by:

[VC] Vasyl Cherepanyn,
[LC] Leontine Coelewij,
[LD] Linda van Deursen,
[OH] Owen Hatherley,
[BH] Brad Haylock,
[DH] Dirk van den Heuvel,
[EJ] Experimental Jetset,
[LL] Lieven Lahaye,
[SM] Samata Masato (Delaware),
[TM] Tom McDonough,
[KM] Kateryna Mishchenko,
[OF] Other Forms (Jack Henrie Fisher & Alan Smart),
[MO] Mark Owens,
[MP] Megan Patty,
[AP] Adam Pendleton,
[SR] Simon Reynolds,
[IS] Ian F. Svenonius,
[MW] McKenzie Wark,
[LW] Lori Waxman,
[MZ] Mimi Zeiger.

Footnotes

1.
Counterstructures

Maybe this is a good place to put the footnote about footnotes? I love them, and have ever since I first read David Foster Wallace, the late American essayist and author of the novel *Infinite Jest*, which famously included 388 endnotes, some of which had their own footnotes. Footnotes tell alternate stories, digressive and tangential stories; they are a drawer for storing the little bits and bobs that need holding onto, but would otherwise be in the way. When I was in graduate school in 2000, I annotated an essay by Rosalind Krauss on Claude Cahun, as an act of scholarly aggression against a text that made me furious in its arrogance and sexism. I wanted to cut it up; instead, I stabbed it with two dozen righteous (and rigorously cited) counterattacks. [LW]

2.
Superstructures
Infrastructures
Substructures
Counterstructures
Destructures
Deconstructures
Constructures
Reconstructures
Macrostructures
Microstructures
Ultrastructures
Hyperstructures
Antistructures

In the mid-20th century, the British architects Alison and Peter Smithson, famed inventors of the New Brutalism, proposed the city had to become a "basic structure," "a system of services and communications to allow for maximum freedom for growth and change." [DH]

3.
The city as an infrastructure for language / Language as an infrastructure for the city

The original version of this text was written in 2017, as an introduction to an exhibition that took place in the beginning of 2018. Invited by RMIT University (Melbourne) to create a retrospective on our own work, we opted for a different kind of exhibition: a large, site-specific installation, in which we focused on four of the modernist tendencies that have greatly influenced and inspired our practice (Constructivism, the Situationist International, the Provo movement, and the Post-Punk condition). In particular, we wanted to explore the way in which these four movements used the city as a platform for language – and conversely, we tried to see how the city manifested itself in the language of each of these movements.

The text thus functioned as a broad introduction, and was incorporated (as printed posters) in the exhibition itself. Within that specific context, it served its purpose.

However, for the context of this publication, we thought the text was too skeletal, too schematic – it certainly lacked a more critical perspective. That's why we decided to invite a broad array of writers to contribute footnotes to our essay – a motley crew of artists, academics, specialists, and generalists. All people whose thinking we admire.

We hope that the footnotes (so generously contributed by these writers) will add some depth and substance to our original text. Moreover, we hope that this collection of footnotes will offer a more fragmented and layered perspective – just as fragmented and layered as modernism itself. [EJ]

4.
The city is a discourse

Understanding and discussing cities, or "the city," as texts or as somehow linguistic has a long history, and has meant a variety of things with a variety of degrees of seriousness in different contexts. To deploy Barthes here, however, points to a specific historical period in which concepts of language as "structural" were being absorbed and digested, both by people working with language – writers and literary critics, anthropologists, social scientists – and by people involved in organizing and constructing "structures" of various sorts – artists, architects, designers, planners, and engineers. One part of this metabolic process would involve a back-projection of structuralist conceptual models onto discourses that were discovered to be already proto-structuralist, most significantly here, Marxist political economy and Freudian psychoanalysis. In all of these translations, traffic across disciplinary boundaries, there were and continue to be friction, resistance, and viscosity in preexisting discourses, and often highly tendentious differences in what things are taken to mean and how imported conceptual schemas were to be to applied to longer-standing issues and established dichotomies.

In architecture, conceptions of a "language of architecture," largely having to do with styles of ornament and visual composition, had been in place since the formulation of neoclassicism in the Renaissance. Somewhat paradoxically, these had managed to be both systems of cultural markers – because language is cultural – and idealist notions of Neoplatonist "pure form," which could have either rationalist or more esoteric connotations. As modernity developed, with architecture deeply embroiled in both the material and symbolic politics of emerging national cultures and globalizing capitalism, these formal languages would be spun into national styles and invested with political and cultural significance, and this would inform a Modernist desire to define an International Style supposedly free of culturally loaded semiotic content, and set free from the nightmare of history.

To the currents in architectural and allied political discourses that had either sought to oppose and resist Modernism or to refigure it as something purely aesthetic or somehow inherently less revolutionary than in the hopes of its most radical proponents, the idea of a turn toward language seemed to offer an opportunity to reject materialism and restore the primacy of symbolic orders and the cultural mythos they support. This conservative, or even explicitly reactionary, conception of "post-modernism" was of course not the only way that architecture and urban space was thought about in structuralist terms. A number of other architects, urbanists, and theorists working both within the framework of Modernism and beyond it, developed ways of understanding the city as either an anthropological social structure, and system of information transmission and exchange, or as a mediating infrastructure for semiotic spatial experience.

It is even possible to conceive of Modernism as set of specific ways that the real and the symbolic, and therefore aesthetics and politics, are seen to be related, and therefore to see the critiques and contestations of Modernism in "postmodernist" discourses, as well as many of its internal (if such interiority can really be imagined) struggles, as attempts to understand and articulate the way that semiotic structures relate to and are manifest in the concrete reality of material culture. The questions which present themselves here are then, what is the value – the utility, the joy, the stakes, the point – of engaging with these historical discourses, and what is the correct, or at least most useful, way of understanding this issue that was itself a conflict in understandings? [OF/AS]

5.
The city is a discourse

Like a little explosion in my brain, Laurie Anderson's voice pops up: "Language. It's a virus! Ooh!"

Is language a structure, too? If so, for sure a slippery one, particularly so in the case of the English variant, and the English word for "structure." I think it was Ludwig Mies van der Rohe who pointed out the profound difference of *Struktur* in the German language from *structure* in English. Another German refugee, the historian Nikolaus Pevsner, cleverly remarked that a bicycle shed may be a building but is not quite architecture. I don't agree. The bicycle figured prominently in Futurist iconography, bicycle wheels were a great inspiration for Duchamp as well as for Constant. Provo's "White Bike Plan" made the revolution a real possibility. Bicycles can still change our cities, also today. [DH]

6.
This environment has to be made human

It seems that this materialist credo was penned by a 24- or 25-year-old Marx, in a paper related to his book *The Holy Family*, co-written with Engels in 1844:

If man receives from the external world and from his experience in the external world all his feelings, ideas, &c., then it is evidently our business to reorganize the empirical world in such a manner that man should only experience the really humane and acquire the habit of it. [...] If man is formed by circumstances, then we must humanize the circumstances. If man is social by nature, then man develops his true nature in society only, and we must measure the power of his nature not by the power of a single individual, but by the power of society.

What this implies is that the modern city, the city shaped by the accumulation of capital and by relationships of exchange – the city that Engels, say, had been exploring during his recent time in England – was precisely not a human environment, was in fact inhuman to the extent that it answered to economic imperatives above all others. To humanize the city would, then, be one of the central tasks of a revolutionary transformation that sought to abolish all alienations. [TM]

7.
Acute awareness

Those Who Believe
shall be Saved,

But!

[SM]

8.
Deep desire

Those Who Doubt
shall not be Saved,

But!

[SM]

9.
To shape those surroundings ourselves

Marx and Engels might be echoing the utopian socialist Charles Fourier there. Fourier designed imaginary built forms for the combination of the passions and for forms of social life that would shed both the family and the state. He's a strong if not always acknowledged influence on many of the other people and movements in this chapter. Fourier's *New Amorous World*, not published until 1967, is a blueprint for the form of a good life, social, sexual, emotional, that is still in advance of many utopian architectures. [MW]

10.
Walls and words

Didn't Charles Baudelaire recognize just this inhumanity to be found in our environment? In his poem "Correspondences," published in Paris about two decades after Marx's reflections, he spoke of the natural world as "a temple where living pillars / Let sometimes emerge confused words; / Man crosses it through forests of symbols / which watch him with intimate eyes."

The poem uses its natural setting as a means to consider that other realm that has excluded the human: the second nature of the city. Walking under the arcades of the Rue de Rivoli or those of the garden of the Palais-Royal, hearing the din of the crowd around him, Baudelaire reimagines the modern city as a "forest of symbols" uttering "confused words." Paris, in the midst of being made over in the image of capital under Baron Haussmann, might be made over again, in language. For its "living pillars," whether advertising columns or classical architecture, speak only symbolically, in code, and must be deciphered by the sensitive wanderer. In the absence of its collective humanization through revolutionary action, the city could be transformed through a series of imaginary projections by the individual artist, fantasies through which the material facticity of architecture and urbanism is remade in words. This is of necessity a melancholic project. As Baudelaire writes in "The Swan": "[...] New palaces, scaffolding, blocks of stone, / Old quarters, all become for me an allegory, / And my dear memories are heavier than rocks." [TM]

11.
Walls and words

The city as semioscape: constantly signifying, offering guidance and instructions, directions and prohibitions.

It's not a property unique to modernity: think of the non-verbal symbols and glyphs used by medieval craftsmen and tradesmen to identify the goods and services provided within. But the modern city is certainly a bombardment of signs, from advertising's triggers to desire (Gang of Four's "coercion of the senses") to the code of the road painted on the tarmac surface itself, as well as elevated signposts.

The population, too, presents itself as a moving text to be read, broadcasting its subdivision into taste tribes and branded micronations of style. To move through the city is to be constantly, if semi-consciously, engaged in the work of identification and interpretation. [SR]

12.
Walls and words

Perhaps it makes more sense now to think that we live no longer just in second nature.

A second nature builds itself out of and against what it retrospectively casts as a primary nature, which then appears ambivalently as a haven from built form but also as a resource. But this can only really be the sensibility of an imperial city, able to command the world as a site of extraction.

Being from mining country myself, every time I see the skyline rising, I imagine the pits being dug down to make it possible. In any case, the infrastructure of the extraction of resources and labor on a planetary scale is now doubled by one that extracts information on a planetary scale – as if it were the oil, coal, and iron ore there for the taking by a new ruling class. Ironically, the city becomes the mining site for this extraction, embedded in a third nature not just of built form but of planetary computation. [MW]

13.
Language lives inside us

"Language. It's a virus!" It spreads, and in its invisible ways it's bigger than us humans for sure; it has a different intelligence while it connects and envelopes us. As Johan Huizinga has pointed out in his *Homo Ludens*, civilization is born in the realm of play: "It does not come from play like a baby detaching itself from the womb: it arises in and as play, and never leaves it." For Huizinga, the ultimate "homo ludens," or playing man, was the poet, the holder of the key to the secret beyond human ratio and emotion, for sure an almost theological understanding of the figure of the poet. [DH]

14.
To speak with Heidegger

What does it mean to "speak with Heidegger" here? Here in the text, and in the here and now of the contemporary situation? I am fortunate enough to have started reading Heidegger as an undergraduate at the University of California Berkeley, with Herbert Dreyfus, who played such an important role in translating Heidegger's work into English, and importing it into the United States, that he was often accused by critics of making Heidegger into his own thought, or essentially "speaking with Heidegger." Dreyfus had a stock story he seemed to greatly enjoy telling, about conducting one of the last interviews that Michel Foucault gave before his death. Committed Heideggerian that he was, Dreyfus asked if Foucault felt that he had been influenced by Heidegger. Committed transgressive rebel that he was – and only more so for being able to give a deathbed confession – Foucault replied that, for all the obvious reasons, young, French, leftist intellectuals of his generation were absolutely forbidden from reading Heidegger, "and so, of course, we read every word."

Our generation of designers, if that is indeed the voice that is speaking here, seem not to be subject to any such prohibitions, or to read with such diligence. What then are these texts to us? Have we really discovered some happy surfactant that can mix up these, originally immiscible, discourses – Marx and Heidegger, Benjamin and Barthes – into a frothy, Sloterdijkian foam? Or if these words are buildings and cities, are these texts ruins? Perhaps they are to be addressed as the wreckage piled upon wreckage that the Angel of History sees continually thrown at its feet, but when, in the next section (spoiler alert!) "we" get to identify with the Angelus Novus, it is in such a bumptious, cowabunga, riders-on-the-storm way, that they seem more like the heroic ruins so beloved by generations of Romantics – pick any path you like, from Hölderlin and Goethe, through Schinkel (and Albert Speer, if you are feeling brutal), to Aldo Rossi and John Hejduk, or whoever the leading lights of the contemporary round of evergreen, gray vs. white false dichotomy, "postmodernism" are – than the absolute catastrophe seen by a brokenhearted, emphatically unheroic, death-haunted, deracinated Jew, who, despite having been almost always a desperate exile running for his life, still managed to look to both the present and the future with brilliant lucidity. [OF/AS]

15.
Poetically, man dwells

The Nazi thinker's notion of "poetically" dwelling referred to the human measure and measure-taking of the cosmos and the earth. To illuminate this idea, he himself referred to the romantic hero of German Idealism, the poet Friedrich Hölderlin. The deconstructing force of the New York performer Laurie Anderson, on the other hand, builds on the work of the closeted gay (bisexual?) Beat Generation author William S.Burroughs. Burroughs appropriated the Dadaist text-cutting technique to compose his renowned masterpiece *Naked Lunch* (1959), which David Cronenberg famously turned into the hallucinating science fiction movie of 1991, with humans metamorphosing into insects and centipedes. *Naked Lunch* was written after Burroughs's novels *Junkie* (1953) and *Queer* (unpublished until 1985), and was the first novel using the technique of cutting-up and re-pasting typed texts. Through this rearranging of words and language, he created something of a place to dwell, I suppose, inside his own language, or at least inside the perversion of the structure of an oppressive language.

The proposition for living inside language also reminds me of quite a different poet, the Dutch Jan Slauerhoff, restless and nomadic, a ship's doctor and famed for his expression "Alleen in mijn gedichten kan ik wonen" (I can only live inside my poems). Was he a Proto-Punk, or Proto-Provo? At the time, reading his short stories and novels when I was a teenager, I was triggered by the connection between language, poetry, and dwelling. Now, today, I am not so much interested in the poetry as such, but more curious about this possessive adjective of "mijn" – this act of reclaiming, of and through language. Acts of appropriation and occupation, as a necessary disruption of the larger structure, to make it your own, and re-own. [DH]

16.
Our cities are poems, our words are buildings

Perhaps, however, it is wrong to write of the material facticity of architecture and urbanism when speaking of the modern city. After all, the transformations Baudelaire experienced in the mid-19th century were those attendant precisely on Paris being remade as spectacle – the undoing of those age-old ties of the quartier, with its complex web of social and economic interactions, and their replacement by an image compounded of long, straight boulevards with their street furniture of kiosks, gas lamps, and the like; a scenography of grand, classicizing monuments terminating vistas; all of it animated by the urban crowd of strollers and shoppers.

There was little "material" about it; Marx describes it rather as something almost spectral. The city's "industry and commerce expanded to colossal dimensions," he writes; "financial swindling celebrated cosmopolitan orgies; the misery of the masses was set off by a shameless display of gorgeous, meretricious, and debased luxury." This spectacle would find its antithesis in the Commune of 1871, which was, among other things, an attempt collectively to rewrite the city: in a language that exploded in its streets and on its walls, in lectures, newspapers, and posters; and in spatial acts of erasure, from the "deflation" of the Vendôme Column to the public burning of the guillotine – "positive voids," the Situationists would later call them – that revised the urban text to produce possible spaces of freedom. [TM]

17.
Our cities are poems, our words are buildings

One of the most famous lines in Reyner Banham's *Los Angeles: The Architecture of Four Ecologies* (1971) is as much about language as it is about the city itself. "I learned to drive in order to read Los Angeles in the original," he writes, comparing himself to other tweedy Brits who learned Italian in order to delve into Dante's hellish depths. By equating mobility with literacy, Banham's quote suggests a particular kind of text – a legato cursive drawn of freeways and onramps and punctuated by strip mall signage and Sunset Strip advertisements.

Indeed, the title card of the 1972 BBC Films production *Reyner Banham Loves Los Angeles* is a billboard designed by Deborah Sussman. The camera zooms in on a bright yellow sign hovering above a parking lot. Sussman's hand-drawn puffy orange and red letters are set amidst an array of similarly puffy clouds. An early employee of the Eames Office, Sussman knew her way around modernism, but her illustration thumbs its nose at such constraints, resembling something scribbled by a lovesick teenager on a spiral notebook while listening to the Carpenters. [MZ]

18.
Maelstrom

The metaphor of the maelstrom, which we used a couple of times in this text, is something we shamelessly borrowed from the great Marxist humanist Marshall Berman (1940–2013) – who, in *All That is Solid Melts into Air* (1982), gave one of the best definitions of modernism ever written:

To be modern is to experience personal and social life as a maelstrom, to find one's world and oneself in perpetual disintegration and renewal, trouble and anguish, ambiguity and contradiction: to be part of a universe in which all that is solid melts into air. To be a modernist is to make oneself somehow at home in the maelstrom, to make its rhythms one's own, to move within its currents in search of the forms of reality, of beauty, of freedom, of justice. [EJ]

19.
Clashing voices

(Main street version)

True is false
Black is white
Gain is loss
New is old
Fast is slow
Hot is cool
Boy is girl
High is low

Heavy is light
Ill is well
Yes is no
Sad is glad
Better is worse

(Back street version)

False is true
White is black
Loss is gain
Old is new
Slow is fast
Cool is hot
Girl is boy
Low is high
Light is heavy
Well is ill
No is yes
Glad is sad
Worse is better

Main is back
Back is main
[SM]

20.
Equal parts optimism and pessimism

[SM]

21.
Possible ways out of the ruins

Modernism began before the catastrophe of the Great War, during a period of relative, if tense, stability. You could make an equally strong argument that modernism prefigured, expressed, harnessed, and even in some cases consciously identified with and exalted the energies of disruption and destabilization. Anticipating the accelerationist school in contemporary philosophy, the Italian Futurists gleefully thrilled to the capacity for ruination that technology opened up in everything from modern warfare to the motorcar (which, as Virilio later argued, simultaneously invented the car crash).

Marinetti and the other future Mussolini fans in the movement exalted the superhuman might that was afforded through merger of man and machine: the way that technology could amplify the will-to-power into a kind of Promethean priapism of the spirit. If the Italian Futurists had certain aesthetic commonalities with the Soviet Constructivists, psychologically and libidinally and politically, Marinetti and his gang were more like Destructivists: less interested in building a new world of peace and plenty, more excited about trampling the old world to smithereens. [SR]

22.
Scratches the surface

Let's recall here Alexander Bogdanov's Bolshevik utopian novel *Red Star*, which imagines a communist utopia on Mars, with quite detailed imaginings of built form, social organization, forms of cybernetic labor. Bogdanov's work was later suppressed, as he had earned Lenin's displeasure even before the October Revolution, but it was influential for a generation of Soviet writers and artists. There's more than a nod to it in Kim Stanley Robinson's *Red Mars* and its sequels. [MW]

23.
Constructivism

Wassily Kandinsky was an influential figure in the early development of Constructivism, but his relationship with the younger generation of Russian artists became increasingly contentious. In the 1999 movie *Double Jeopardy*, Elizabeth "Libby" Parsons discovers the alias of her husband (who had faked his own murder – a crime for which she was framed) through the auction records on the fictitious "Art scan" website: it shows that the 1911 Kandinsky *Study for the Cover of "Der Blaue Reiter" Almanac*, previously owned by Nicholas "Nick" Parsons, was last sold by a certain "Jonathan Devereaux."

When Travis Lehman, Libby's rogue parole officer, meets Jonathan Devereaux, he glances over the paintings in his office, signaling to the viewer that he now believes Libby's claim about the fake murder.

Travis Lehman: "Those are nice pictures… did your kids do 'em?"
Jonathan Devereaux, aka Nicholas "Nick" Parsons: "Uhm, no, those pictures are by a very great artist named Kandinsky"
Travis Lehman: "Oh…"
Jonathan Devereaux, aka Nicholas "Nick" Parsons: "But... why do I think you already knew that..." [LL]

24.
Esoteric acronyms

So here we are, still living amongst these ruins. They seem to be other peoples' ruins, or at least definitely not our fault. We are trying to get through, or out, and yet "somehow" we are still managing to develop new aesthetic "languages." Now we are trying to identify not with a metaphorical angel but with real people: Soviet Communist revolutionaries of a hundred years ago. It is difficult. They are strange, and they lived a long time ago in a world where politics and aesthetics were radically different in both force and form. They also associated and worked together in arrangements we find strange, which they named with acronyms and abbreviations, as if they were industry groups, military units, government agencies. From the vantage point of our contemporary situation, these appear "occult" and "esoteric," as if, like technology, politics that is sufficiently advanced also becomes indistinguishable from magic. Do we mean this, though? Is it really the case that shop-jobbing graphic designers of the early 21st century, who know only corporations, "limited liability partnerships," find it deliriously arcane to imagine design being the work of a revolutionary brigade, or a collectivized factory, while remaining perfectly comfortable with such profane necromancy as the concept of corporate personhood? Are these people, who worked and struggled so hard to draw these distinctions – between Constructivism and Productivism, between realism and abstraction, between the symbolic and the material – and who would kill and die for them, really to be consigned together to a single "whirlpool" like so many eccentric, "passionate" geniuses and holy fools?

Again, the stakes of this question seem to lie less in what is proper or correct – respectful of the victims, holding the perpetrators accountable, "doing justice" to the achievements of these artists – and is more about what lessons can be drawn from this and what practical use this history is to serve in contemporary practice. How do today's style wars serve as proxies for "culture war" politics, translate to concrete reality "on the street," and how is this to be understood in relation to Soviet Modernism, where a cataclysmic, real revolution, and the catastrophic real civil war that followed, precipitated a cultural revolution translated into and played out through conflicts between aesthetic styles?

One figure that stands out from this maelstrom, like a human finger in a bowl of solyanka soup, is Sergei Tretyakov, of the Productivist LEF group. Like Mayakovsky, Tretyakov was a writer and poet, and like Mayakovsky, experimented in writing on walls. In his exegesis on writing in the Soviet Union, "The Author as Producer," Benjamin sites Tretyakov's work as an example of revolutionary technique, that overcomes the "sterile opposition between form and content." Frustrated with the inability of his conventional writing practice to effectively contribute to the material work of building a new society, Tretyakov had moved to a collective farm and developed a form of "wall novels," that he would write in episodes on the wall of the collective meeting hall, so that workers returning from the fields would be able to read a new installment of the story every evening. The wall novels combined literary narrative with useful and relevant practical information about modern, mechanized, collective agriculture, but what is more important in Benjamin's account is the way that they "refunction" the form of writing and engage it with the material transformations of revolutionary society. Benjamin contrasts this transformation of the apparatus of production by revolutionary artists with the work of "hacks" who, however radical the content they produce is, refuse to alienate the relational forms of production from the bourgeoise, but are instead content to "eternally to draw new effects from the political situation in order to amuse the public." If it is the case that Mayakovsky's poetry kiosks can be understood as architecture made into writing, or the scope of writing expanded to include architecture and urban space, then it is worth considering whether Tretyakov's alienation of the novel by turning writing into architecture is the same, or actually an exact opposite or mirror image, and what in all of this is affirmation and what is negation.

Tretyakov is an especially bitter figure to remember, however, because despite his deep commitment and the courage of his radicalism, he was convicted of writing a play that undermined the "Russian family" and sent to his death in the gulag. Mayakovsky also died under suspicious circumstances, either by hopeless suicide or by a secret execution made to look like a suicide, and Benjamin would also kill himself when he felt that he could no longer escape his fascist pursuers. Over and over in the 1930s, both in the Soviet Union and in the West, the hacks win, and the progressive revolutionaries meet with early death, or at best, defeat and frustrated obscurity. [OF/AS]

25.
Esoteric acronyms

Indeed, the mystical and occult dimensions of modernism more broadly have only begun to be explored. See, especially, *Le Corbusier and the Occult* (Cambridge, MA: MIT Press, 2009) and Elizabeth Otto, *Haunted Bauhaus* (Cambridge, MA: MIT Press, 2019). [MO]

26.
Esoteric acronyms

Proletkult was a little different to the other avant-gardes. Bogdanov was its instigator, and its project was nothing less than the organization of the working class as the generator of its own knowledge. He saw it as a necessary counterbalance to the power of the party and the unions in the early configuration of Soviet power. Bogdanov's mission is still a striking one: what would the organization, from the bottom up, of the knowledge and art of all the working peoples look like? Could there be a comradely production of knowledge without claims to sovereignty by one form of knowledge over all the others? Not surprisingly, this ran counter to Lenin's thinking, where the party was supposed to stand over and above all other forms of knowledge. One might think this issue is dead history, but the People's Republic of China is still run by an information-age descendant of Lenin's form of the party. [MW]

27.
The city

In *The City*, the first urban novel in Ukrainian literature, written by Valerian Pidmohylnyi in 1927, the urban space formed a landscape of the Soviet New Economic Policy. This brief period of economic revival, which was also perhaps the golden age of Ukrainian culture, came to an end in the 1930s when NEP was replaced by Stalinism.

The protagonist, Stepan Radchenko, arrives in Kyiv by steamer along the Dnipro. Disoriented and bothered by the city at first, he constantly returns to the familiar shoreline to cook food on an open fire and to wash. This Robinson seems in no hurry to explore unknown lands. But gradually the city ceases to be a tangible island, and instead, with its "rolling crowds" and boundless streets, to him Kyiv becomes a force of nature. Stepan internalizes the city landscape, and the orphaned young villager – the typical Soviet new man – imagines himself as an oblivious wave flowing through a future life. From time to time he crashes into small private enclaves, be it the modest rooms of his mistresses or the apartments of members of the old academic community, whose homes, after all the revolutionary requisitions, resembled an "island following an earthquake." In these spaces Stepan senses the imminent death of the remnants of pre-revolutionary oppression. He willingly projects his political ressentiment onto himself, without remorse cutting off his village friends, along with his new city girlfriends and privileged acquaintances, once he no longer needs them in his life.

His time of extreme dis-engagement is one of active creative production. The Kyiv lights form a constellation that Stepan now recognizes. He transforms his personal experience in the civil war into literature. But once the distant past is exhausted, the recent past in Kyiv begins to exhaust Stepan himself. The city space contracts and is filled with ghosts of discarded friends. Ultimately, Stepan manages to reconcile with them, look into the "city's dark abyss," and continue to write.

The City is a psychological novel that paints the protagonist's inner landscape. But along with Stepan, isolated from everything and everyone, there is another character – time. "I kiss this day" is one of Stepan's most poetic phrases. These words conceal the temporality of the liberation period in Soviet history, which I would call a time of island-like conditioning.

An island briefly surfaced, felt the touch of hundreds of coastal waves, and went back under water, leaving behind a blink of art and political hope. [KM]

28.
Urban environment

In *Postmodernism, or, The Cultural Logic of Late Capitalism*, Frederic Jameson argues that modernism emerged at a time when industrial modernity is a rapidly expanding but still relatively circumscribed enclave within a socioeconomic reality still largely defined by the agricultural and pastoral. That is the backdrop against which modernism derives its libidinal charge, its polemical salience, its sense of itself as vanguard. To deify the motorcar, as Marinetti did, only makes sense at a time when the horse remains the principal mechanism of transportation and haulage. When the internal combustion engine achieves dominance and omnipresence, it necessarily becomes commonplace; it can no longer signify as harbinger of the future, because it's the everyday now.

There is an implicit antipathy to the rural within Soviet modernism that paralleled the Communist state's increasingly antagonistic relationship with the peasantry, and in particular with the well-off kulak class, who were regarded as nest-feathering counter-revolutionaries. The land and the people who cultivated it symbolized Russia's feudal past (barely a half-century earlier, peasant serfs had still been virtually the chattels of lordly landowners). Agriculture stood for the inertia of tradition, for faith and a fatalistic acceptance of one's allotted place in the caste system. The Five-Year Plans of accelerated industrialization aimed to force the country forward into an urban future: the rapid post-revolution development of an industrial sector would build the proletariat suitable for the new era (an inversion of Marx, for whom industrialization was the prerequisite to the emergence of revolutionary thinking at the site of production, the organization of labor, etc.). Soviet modernism's stylistic savagery offered an aesthetic corollary to the brutal treatment of the kulaks and the forced collectivization of agriculture. The graphic language of Constructivism and Suprematism slices through the organicism of preceding art, its stark lines and abstracted blocs of primary color breaking with the curvilinear and the chiaroscuro.

A similar technophile and anti-bucolic impetus animated the Italian Futurists, who equated their country's landscape of olive groves and terracotta farmhouses with the changeless and the abiding. The unhurried rhythms of rustic life, the proximity to animals and Nature, the peace and quiet represented everything static and sluggish in the culture. So they poured scorn on "the holy green silence" and even mischievously proposed abandoning the starchy, soporific national dish of pasta with a stern new cuisine made of inedible substances like perfumed sand. [SR]

29.
Spatial poem

Different But Similar
(stereo mix)

L – Parsley, sage, rosemary
& thyme
R – John, Paul, George & Ringo

L – Spacecraft Discovery One
R – Overlook Hotel

L – Vegan Burger & Fried Potato
R – Sherlock Holmes
& Dr. Watson

L – Tempeh, Lettuce & Tomato
R – Marieke, Erwin & Danny

L – Language
R – City
[SM]

30.
Language as a place to dwell in

Cometbus is a fanzine, written by Aaron Cometbus and published intermittently since 1981. Most of the text is set in his own handwriting, always in all caps. A telltale sign of his handwriting is how the horizontal lines of double capital T's (i.e., TT) are always connected, making it look like the letter pi from the greek alphabet (i.e., TT). Aaron is currently the co-owner of a Brooklyn secondhand bookshop called Book Thug Nation. You can tell by the handwritten sign for the category "ESSAYS, LETTERS, LIT. CRIT." [LL]

31.
Smoking chimneys

Again, compare with the Italian Futurists, whose aesthetic war against the Romantic cult of the pre-industrial pastoral past was waged on all artistic fronts. Luigi Russolo was generalissimo of a Futurist campaign to reinvent music by embracing sound production methods more aligned with the industrial era, by devising timbres and effects that reflected the urban soundscape better than the traditional acoustic instrumentation of the orchestra. To implement his theories about a new "art of noises," Russolo invented the Intonarumori (which roughly translates as "noise-intoning machines"). His arsenal included the Gorgogliatore ("gurgler"), which generated a metallic rustle, and the Ululatore ("hooter"), which sounds like a vacuum cleaner with something stuck in its pipe. Marinetti, for his part, relied on his own vocal apparatus to create onomatopoeic sound-poetry compositions like "La Guerra" and "La Battaglia Di Adrianopoli," which mimicked the siege cannons and machine guns of the Balkan Wars. [SR]

32.
Smoking chimneys

Andrei Platonov imagined a "factory of facts" for the collaborative production of literature, with a division of labor among different kinds of writer. It was different to that art which borrowed the aesthetic of the factory. Like the productivists, it was about changing its form. Platonov also had a lot to say about built form, for example, in his famous novel *Chevengur*, which is about a small village cooperative, one of the things that happened while nobody was watching too closely during the civil war. His *Foundation Pit* is a bitter indictment of the party's Stalinist obsession with construction. Workers wear themselves out digging an ever-bigger foundation pit for a superstructure that could never exist. [MW]

33.
Para-architecture in itself

Who accommodates what, actually?

Conventionally, architects assume that their structures support and accommodate life. Among others, Herman Hertzberger has formulated this idea as the basis for the social obligation of architecture. But perhaps it might be quite the opposite? That the events of life bring architecture into being?

I had to think of this when I was waiting at Schiphol airport and watched a Boeing 747 arriving at the gate, the ultimate icon of late 20th-century globalization. Because of the raised cockpit, the plane always impressed me as a friendly giant animal. Locking onto the pier, the animal-like structure opened up all sorts of body parts and a flurry of smaller machine-animals started to service the big creature, like a crocodile opening his jaws to let in the birds who will clean its teeth.

The human body is inhabited by about 1.5 kilograms of viruses, bacteria, fungi, and other microbes. It is not just that the human body "houses" those micro-ecologies. Without them, the human body would actually collapse and die. Buildings and cities, too, without people, die and turn to dust. Those ecologies support us. Until they start proliferating and overwhelm us. Ecology is not quite like paradise. [DH]

34.
Historical photos of this oversized maquette

I went and looked up these photos, having only seen the indoor ones of the tower, and they remind me of nothing so much as a good old Eastern Orthodox procession. That might seem too ironic, but really the church got something fundamentally right with their ritualized group walks: there's nothing like moving through a city, all together now, with large items of symbolic significance in tow.

It's a ready-made formula for all sorts of occasions where collective sentiment is foremost: political protests, American Thanksgiving Day parades, even a series of gleeful circumambulations scored by the Fluxus artist Erik Andersen. In one iteration of his *Idle Walks*, at the 1985 Festival of Fanatics in Roskilde, Denmark, 30 people (half of them part of the performance troupe Berzerk, the other half onlookers) wove through town wearing a single monumental blue garment sewed intermittently with a cap, vest, arm, or leg. [LW]

35.
Models turn into buildings, buildings into models

What kinds of models exist? When are buildings no longer models?

There are many forms of building between model and realization. In 1968, shortly after the assassination of Martin Luther King Jr., an encampment called Resurrection City stood for six weeks on the National Mall in Washington, D.C. Organized by the Southern Christian Leadership Conference (SCLC) under the leadership of the late Dr. King, this city-within-a-city was one of the major actions of the SCLC's Poor People's Campaign, an effort to build a nationwide multiracial coalition of poor Americans.

Resurrection City was composed of over 3,000 inhabitants and hundreds of plywood and fabric tents supported by two-by-fours. The buildings were schematic DIY structures, to which citizens attached spray-painted language, graphics, and images. The city was a fifteen-acre draft, under continuous revision: a collectively authored urban community. Some of the most memorable images from Resurrection City are not of the protest actions and the crowds, but of the buildings and their simple, abstract frames in the process of being erected and annotated, and, later, dismantled by police.

That this form of city would prove to be impossible or unsustainable, and that its demands failed to yield immediate results was, in a sense, not exceptional. What emerged from the experiment, however briefly, was a class solidarity that American parties and identitarian politics could not or would not provide: from bare frames, a polyphonic voice. [AP]

36.
Dreams unfulfilled

Russian revolutionaries looked back on the Commune as the great 19th-century precedent for their own enormous social experiment – even as the Bolshevik bureaucracy regarded its radical democracy with profound suspicion, if not contempt. In 1929 the young filmmakers Grigori Kozintsev and Leonid Trauberg set about a project that could be considered a filmic adaptation of *The Civil War in France*, Marx's account of the Commune, written in the immediate aftermath of its suppression. *The New Babylon*, as their film was called, tells of the class struggle at the heart of the Commune by overlaying Marxist analysis with a romantic tale of doomed love between a shop-assistant-cum-Communard and a soldier of the reactionary Versailles army. "The New Babylon" was the name of the modern department store – clearly modeled on Zola's account of transformations in mid-19th-century commerce in *Au Bonheur des Dames* – where the main character works.

The store is a synecdoche for all the bourgeois corruptions of Second Empire Paris – a veritable altar to the commodity fetish and its spectacular staging, a contemporary instantiation of that wicked city of Biblical lore, place of subaltern captivity and exile. The collective action of the Commune is its inversion, of course, but we should read Kozintsev and Trauberg's choice of title as naming more than just the venality of capital: hadn't the Communards, like the Babylonians of old with their tower, attempted to "storm the heavens"? Their film's title, then, points in two directions, looking back to the alienation of the old world while simultaneously anticipating the new, humanized one being collectively fabricated. [TM]

37.
Unrealized

There are a set of frames through which the utopian socialist architecture of the 20th century – and especially, Constructivism – is generally interpreted. The first is *impossibility*; there was no way that anything so crazy and ambitious could possibly have happened, which makes the whole enterprise faintly silly and infantile. The second is *potentiality* – a less scornful version of the former, where the scale of the ambition and the implausibility of its realization is considered a strength rather than a weakness, a sign of the world-transformative potential of the Communist Idea that doesn't need to be tested in actually existing conditions. The third and most popular in recent years is *ruins*, where for the first time it is acknowledged that a large quantity of 1920s Constructivist architecture, and later, architecture of the 1950s–1980s substantially inspired by the Constructivists, was actually built, and inhabited, in places ranging from the USSR itself to Yugoslavia and Britain and Japan. Yet the apparent introduction of lived experience and history into the discourse is quickly wrenched away, by stressing not the actual inhabitation of the Constructivist buildings, but their destroyed and ruined condition, and the apparent or alleged absence of people. All of these can be found to one degree or another in this text, and very few people who have written about Constructivism from the left have avoided them entirely – I know I haven't, when I have written about them myself, particularly the *potentiality* and *ruins* tropes. But perhaps there are ways of looking at Constructivism which stress something different – that concentrate on what happens when the utopian socialist idea begins to be constructed within existing reality – within and against it, as it were?

The more extreme versions of Constructivist architecture were indeed unbuilt and unbuildable – the famous point that there was not enough steel in Russia during the Civil War to build a steel model of Tatlin's Tower, let alone to actually build it in reality, comes most obviously to mind. But the second project of Tatlin and his collective, as Christina Kaier points out in her book *Imagine No Possessions*, was for a more functional kitchen stove. We've known now for some decades that architects and designers trained in UNOVIS or INKhUK and working in VKhUTEMAS managed to get a huge quantity of buildings actually built – most of them between the economic recovery that began in 1923 and 1932, when independent artistic, architectural, and literary groups were officially abolished. Much of it was quite cheaply realized modern architecture, Bauhaus on a minuscule budget, constructed with wood and stucco treated to look like steel and concrete – but a lot of it was every bit as ambitious as the "paper architecture" of the era. The Workers Clubs in Moscow, designed by Konstantin Melnikov and Ilya Golosov; the Palaces of Culture in Moscow and Baku by the Vesnin Brothers; the Factory Kitchens in Leningrad, by a collective that included some of Tatlin's collaborators on the Tower; communal apartments in numerous cities, most famously the Narkomfin collective house in the center of Moscow; the dramatic concrete fortresses of the government centers in Kharkiv and Minsk; the new "socialist cities" in the suburbs of Nizhny Novgorod, Zaporizhia, and the new towns like Magnitogorsk; Constructivist factories everywhere from Baku to Kazan. To name just a few. Some of these are now reasonably well known, thanks to books like Richard Pare's *The Lost Vanguard* – though that book, beautiful and comprehensive as it is, tends to treat these places as if they're depopulated, disused, or ruined. In my experience, this is seldom the case. A typical example here might be the Factory Kitchens in what is now (again) St. Petersburg – ruined in Pare's photographs, today they're well-used, but subdivided between leisure centers, international chains, semi-formal markets, and local youth clubs and canteens. They still function substantially as the "social condensers" they were always envisaged as, albeit in a new and hostile context.

So what I propose for future analyses of Constructivism is a project where we forget the paper architecture, and try instead to uncover the lived histories of the avant-garde. What happens when generations of people have lived in utopian socialist structures? How have they adapted the structure? How has the structure adapted them? There are some examples of this project already taking place: Michal Murawski's research on "still socialist" social condensers in Poland and Russia; Victor Buchli's *Archaeology of Socialism*, on the Narkomfin building; and the research on Ukrainian socialist cities by Ievgeniia Gubkina, to name just three. If we delve into these lived histories, we will find a lot of failure, for sure. Communism never came, the millennium never came to pass, the revolution was betrayed, and you can read that on the subdivided insides and the patchwork facades. But we would also find many examples of what William Morris, talking about London's parks, called "fragments" and "instalments" of a better society, working pretty well. Most of the Workers Clubs are still Workers Clubs. Some of the canteens are still canteens. Look hard enough, and you'll even find some communes that are still communes. How have they survived? How have they held out? What can we learn from them, as designers, architects, and socialists? [OH]

38.
Actual architecture

The iconoclasm of memory: decommunization and its discontents.

A specter is haunting Europe – the specter of communism. All the powers of old Europe have entered into a holy alliance to exorcise this specter: Merkel and Putin, Orbán and Macron, right-wing radicals and Brexiteers. From "decommunization" in Ukraine and Poland to Germany's "Die DDR hat's nie gegeben" (the GDR has never existed) to authoritarian regimes in Russia and Turkey to ruling populists in the Czech Republic and the

United States – communism seems to be treated and fought against as if it was not a symbolic remnant from the half-forgotten period before the proclaimed "end of history," but a living ideological enemy still present on the political agenda.

It is this anti-communism without communists that serves as a common negative signifier of all political trends usually gathered today under the term "illiberalism." What are the social drives of such a widespread ressentiment? How is declared de-communization paving the path to neofascism normalizing newly emerged avatars of the old hatred? Why is it needed in today's entourage of anti-migrant consensus and anti-Semitic backlash? The iconoclastic process of decommunization mirrors the European unconscious in its present mode as an ideology that gained significance, particularly in Eastern Europe, over the last decades.

The fall of the Berlin Wall, a symbol of the Cold War, and the end of European state socialism 30 years ago evoked a historically unique transition from socialism to capitalism, celebrated as a shift to a dynamic network system of power. However, the disintegration of the Socialist Bloc has led to the global dominance of the ideology of financial capitalism. Post-communist transition resulted in growing inequalities, expanding state apparatuses, triumphant nationalism, and new types of physical and electronic walls that sprung up around the globe. The promise of Velvet Revolutions to overcome the historical division and political isolation of Europe's east has been turned into the fortification of Europe; obsessed with border control, this became the main topos of the state of exception today.

The collapse of the Second World meant the general loss of the political alternative to capitalism, when revolutionary or reformist emancipatory projects have been put into the black box of "the end of history." Paradoxically, the infamous acronym TINA (There Is No Alternative), coined by Margaret Thatcher, has become a sort of self-fulfilling prophecy – nowadays, we really find ourselves in a historical period, when probably for the first time there is no political alternative to the global logic of capitalism on the horizon whatsoever. And what we observe is just extremely growing authoritarianism and a new right-wing consensus – there is no far right anymore, it is now in the political mainstream.

Indeed, communism became literally a specter – emptied out, disembodied, a signifier without signified. After 1989–1991, it is not the future but the past that appeared to be highly unpredictable. The basic characteristics of the so-called post-communist condition have been repressing the memory of communism and anti-fascist struggle, and this applies to political subjects worldwide. They have been obsessively concentrated on the past, on memory wars, acting out social frustrations through history, that exactly mark the direction where anger and disillusionment have been channeled after the crash of "really existing socialism." Though, this memory politics is not so much about the communist past, it is rather the present and future political and economic hegemony, in Europe in particular, which is at stake.

Memory discourse presents a crucial dimension of the current global constellation smoothening the dominant politics of waging wars and erecting walls on the ideological level, functioning actually as a fetish. Remarkably, this politics of memory has nothing to do with history – it's not about how to remember, but how to forget. It is a hybrid memory, to use the term commonly applied to the modern type of war, that has politics of fear as its other side and goes much deeper than Nietzsche's "what unites us is not what we remember, but what we together decided to forget." Today, it is more radical: what unites us is what has never happened, but what we together decided to remember as if it had. This shift to an illusionary past in the situation, when the only future available is dystopian, results in thanatological politics which use dead bodies as a political weaponry.

The post-communist situation is generally characterized by various forms of "returning" to imagined roots. The very basic definition of the post-Soviet is simply skipping the Soviet, jumping over the traumatic Soviet experience, trying to reach some authentic national basis. The post-communist society is directed not towards the future; it escapes to the past, to the pre-revolutionary (i.e., the October Revolution) stage "before communism." Such attempts of establishing a founding national myth are usually based on false historical projections: this isolationistic backwardness is a dead-end in the ontological sense; it's a nostalgia for what has never happened. Dictum: we are who we are, not because of the immediate past that made us, but because of the far past we imagined. Politics of memory appeared as a new civic religion stuck in the past continuous.

The ideology of de-communization took a harsh and violent form in Ukraine during recent years, in the context of war and nationalist discursive dominance as one of its outcomes. Russian military intervention and occupation has poisoned the atmosphere inside the country, creating the conditions for political reaction. War has emerged as a political and economic system of relations between the state and the society, becoming an excuse for any unlawful action or inaction that can be justified under the guise of "patriotism" and "protecting the state," wiping out dissent and alternative political agendas from the public space. The logic of war replicates itself in various forms, and decommunization has basically been Ukraine's version of counter-propaganda to oppose the Kremlin's media war on the symbolic level.

After the Maidan revolution and Russian military occupation in 2014, the realm of memory has also been occupied by militarism and political reaction. Decommunization as a specific state policy was in no way some expected answer to a societal request, but at first a far-right initiative supported soon by the state and imposed afterwards from above. Notably, the intention of decommunization applies only to symbolic space, it does not presume any restitution or compensation to victims. The discourse of historical politics is smoothly combined with populism; it's an ersatz for social politics along with imposing austerity measures and reconstructing neo-feudal oligarchic structures of governing. Decommunization itself as essentially a desperate attempt to take revenge on the past is a substitute for justice and the rule of law. Not by occasion the justice system is currently under severe attack in Poland, and is totally non-functional in terms of its basic purpose in Ukraine.

Communist memory has been hotted up, and in the city space, decommunization takes the form of destroying the imagery and monuments inherited from the socialist past. Communist memorials are still difficult to integrate into the nation-state framework; they remain as constantly disturbing sites of discontent. Over the last years, Ukraine has become a country of empty pedestals and erased monuments. It is an *interregnum* period in the monuments' history, when the old idols are gone and the new ones haven't arrived yet, though we are already getting some commemorative substitutes or nationalist replacements. The most ideologically loaded site in that regard today is, perhaps, the former monument to Lenin on Bessarabska Square in central Kyiv – that's where the so-called Leninfall, the demolition of Lenin's monuments throughout the country, started in December 2013. In its current condition it is just a pedestal, without sculpture, with the inscription "LENIN" on it. In a schizophrenical manner, the presence of the word doesn't disturb in the absence of the (destroyed) image – it stays, as if unseen, a real blind spot, a specter, the presence of the absence.

Footnotes

The wave of erasing the traces and hints of the socialist past that swept across East European countries over the last decades usually presented communism as an alien phenomenon imposed by "occupiers" against the nation's will. Although Ukraine, for instance, was shaped as a state in its current (occupied) borders within the Soviet Union, such politics of memory always presume a nation-victim narrative: through distancing from the "false" history, it deprives itself from the moral agency, attempting to get an alibi, not to hold responsibility for the past crimes. On the political market of sufferings, the respective status of victim grants a desirable recognition. "Patriotic" populism externalizes the Soviet period and retroactively nationalizes historical memory, using the communist past for redistribution of political and symbolic capital today.

Together with Soviet memorials, the modernist avant-garde tradition is being wiped out from the public space as a disturbing symbol for counter-memories and alternative historical narratives. Ukrainian socialist culture of the 1920s, after being forcefully provincialized and ruralized in the Russian Empire, brought forth a prominent urban avant-garde movement called the Red Renaissance. It is also dubbed as the Shot Renaissance, referring to a literary and artistic generation destroyed by the Stalin's regime in the 1930s. Actually, it was the last time Ukrainian culture experienced an assault of that scale before today's decommunization, which repeats this gesture in the very same way that it tries to overturn it. This modernist epoch contains a real emancipative potential – it was the most *modern* period in the history of Ukrainian culture. What we can learn from it is something challenging for today's status quo, that is, how to be *contemporary*. Decommunization is a continuation of war by other means, a war against being modern.

This repression of memory results in the revenge of memory in all new forms of social destruction. Ukrainian society is in an extremely traumatized condition; it is a complex layering of both past and recent traumas. Soviet repressions, a wild capitalist "transition" period that produced oligarchy, the permanent absence of social and legal justice, revolutionary violence, war – all of them remain unresolved, overlapping and superimposed on each other. Society is being kept as their hostage; its sensitivity is eroded together with its constantly increasing rejection of all new cases of violence and death. The regressive politics of memory lays the grounds for conflicts that will tear the social fabric to pieces in the future, widening the funnel of violence and pulling the whole society into it, for which it becomes harder and harder to come to its senses and to its own memory.

The iconoclastic drive of decommunization is profoundly self-aggressive – one has to really hate one's mirror image to the extent that the first reaction at hand is disfiguring or demolishing, which is a form of inverted hatred. The lack of capabilities to tackle the evident threats that surpass us in (military) strength redirects frustrated violence onto a safe enemy, the role assigned in this case to the corpse of communism. However, one of the symptomatic developments of the decommunization course conducted country-wide is that being initially aimed at the Soviet memorials does not mean that other monuments remain untouched. The genie was out of the bottle, and we have experienced violations and attacks also on various Polish, Jewish, and Ukrainian memorials, and even Maidan commemoration sites, conducted by different people – just because it became possible and somehow unpunishable. The iconoclastic parcel of decommunization got back to its sender.

Ultimately, one has to ask a seemingly apparent question, which, though, clearly shows where fascism is particularly coming from nowadays: why is the far right in the east of Europe much more severe and harsh than in the west? In that regard, one usually gets a typical finger-pointing game delegating all xenophobic "fascistoid" evil to the periphery and its past, but it is actually quite the opposite. The harshness of the far right in Eastern Europe derives not from the communist past but from the brutality of the fight against that past. We have indeed entered strange political times – we've got plenty of fascists, but no communists. The more decommunization one conducts, the more hardcore neo-Nazi one will get.

Contributing to the political conditions and conception of a social order, where fascism *per se* would be impossible, might be called communism in the past. Today, one could begin with anti-decommunization; that would be a good start. [VC]

39. New Babylon

After CoBrA's acrimonious dissolution in the early 1950s, Constant moved to Paris, spending time there and in a number of other cities on the Continent and across the Channel. He recalls a season passed in Frankfurt in 1951, in a city still pockmarked with bomb craters, and in 1952 he visited London, where the frenetic pace of postwar reconstruction left similar, indelible memories. These images of urban ruination and rebuilding – products of processes of capital accumulation – were the motivation to ask whether the city could be recreated with human rather than economic needs in mind. Could we leave behind our urban prehistory and collectively construct a really humane habitat? The visionary planning project he began a few years later offered a glimpse of this future, a "science fiction of architecture," as his colleague Jorn once called it. When Constant brought his designs to Debord, he proposed they be called "Dériville" – roughly, Drift City, after the Situationist technique of urban wandering; inhabitants of these megastructures were, after all, intended to spend their days and nights at play, drifting through ever-changing ambiances and flexible spaces that could be remade at will. Debord, however, had another suggestion: "New Babylon," which, in its evocation of the biblical tower as symbol of a humanity attempting to realize its own potential against heaven-mandated limits, had a peculiarly Benjaminian ring to it, conjoining, as it does, deep past and utopian future in a single, dialectical image. [TM]

40.
Purges, expulsions, and exclusions

The parting of ways with Dutch artist Constant is a particular loss, and for me the failure of the Situationist International turns on its inability to synthesize certain leading practices of the time, including Constant's. His *New Babylon* is an advanced utopian imaginary, planetary in scale. It is a utopia, not at the level of the city, but at that of a whole infrastructure. It is a properly Marxist utopia that thinks in a quite literal way about base and superstructure. A base made for the production of a free surplus calls for the imagining of superstructures for free play, without the constraints of private property. It is one of the central works of the situationists. [MW]

41.
The urban environment was to be read as a text

In 2020 the inter-connectedness of the global village is acutely felt, but with a foreboding inflection. In the last decade of the previous millennium, however, globalization had different connotations. Then, in the loosely consistent collective imaginary of the Left, the term was synonymous with neoliberal economics and was exemplified by key non-state actors such as the World Bank, the World Trade Organization, and the International Monetary Fund, and by a number of high-profile, controversial free trade agreements, most notably the 1994 North American Free Trade Agreement (NAFTA). In that moment, the city was contested both as a physical site and as an image: a place of increasingly dense cohabitation and palpable gentrification, a symbol of growth won through exploitation but also a canvas for a possibly better future. A number of distinctly urban collective action movements arose, which sought to lay claim to public space as such, or which strove to instantiate better ways of occupying the city. Sustained in duration and characterized by an ethic of non-violence and play, these movements were unlike issue-specific protest marches that characterized prior decades, or riots arising at flashpoints, such as the contemporaneous 1992 Los Angeles uprising.

One of most important urban collective action movements of the time, and perhaps most influential upon later actions and movements, was Reclaim the Streets (RTS). Beginning in London in 1991, but seen around the world by the end of the decade and persistently active in Sydney to this day, RTS is best known for its street parties, with a festive spirit inspired by the UK rave scene. Equal parts party and protest, an RTS event typically sees an intersection or a city block taken over for a number of hours, invariably featuring sound systems but occasionally also other forms of entertainment, such as bouncing castles. Although its earliest roots lay in protests against new roads, and although a number of its instances continue to be aligned with specific local matters, such as labor actions or protests against inappropriate development, RTS quickly became a form of resistance against contemporary capitalism in general. The lineage from RTS to the later Occupy movement is clear, but in the intervening years another collective action movement saw the streets occupied in a different way.

Critical Mass is, or was, a collective bicycle ride, sometimes described as a protest but more often as a celebration. From its beginnings in San Francisco in 1992, Critical Mass grew to become a worldwide movement by the end of the decade. Regular bicycle commuters, couriers, racers, and occasional cyclists would come together on bicycles of all types for a mass ride, usually in the early evening on the last Friday of the month, in major cities around the world, typically with bright colors, bells, whistles, streamers, portable sound systems, and a festive spirit. Numbers would range from a few dozen riders in the smallest cities to a few thousand in the largest, in celebration of the bicycle as a sustainable mode of urban transport, in support of improved infrastructure for cycling and increased driver awareness, and in protest against the prioritization of the automobile in most contemporary urban planning. The biggest events to use the Critical Mass name, on Earth Day and International Car Free Day in Budapest, attracted up to 80,000 riders in the first decade of the new millennium, but the rides had died out in most cities by the middle of the 2010s.

The basic logic of Critical Mass is that of safety in numbers. The group moves at an unhurried pace and tries to avoid being split up. The front of the group stops if it reaches a red light, so as to not ride into crossing traffic, but otherwise the ride does not stop for traffic signals. Riders from the front of the group peel off to block or "cork" intersections, halting automobiles on cross streets with bodies and bikes, and seek to engage drivers in friendly conversation about sustainable transport, often sharing flyers about Critical Mass. These "corkers" rejoin the end of the group when the mass has passed through. So goes the refrain: "We're not blocking traffic, we *are* traffic!"

Part of the historical significance of Critical Mass and RTS lies with the fact that they are early examples of the use of the internet for organizing social action. Printed materials promoting the events were certainly numerous and important, but the development of these movements ran alongside that of then-new communication channels such as email and bulletin boards. Surely the catchily assertive names of Critical Mass and Reclaim the Streets – akin to brand names – also contributed to their impact and reach, and prefigured, too, the memetic force of Occupy, the women's movement Reclaim the Night, and, more recently, the #MeToo movement.

When riding a bicycle through a city at a leisurely pace, as one among a large group of cyclists, it feels as if the whole city has slowed down. Space unfolds as never before, and one notices previously unseen details on buildings, trees, signs, the refraction of light down an alley, and expressions on the faces of passersby. This is, as the controversial anarchist Hakim Bey would say, a temporary autonomous zone, albeit a moving one. Seen from the point of view of the Mass, the geography of the city is momentarily different – a *dérive*, *en masse*, on two wheels. [BH/MP]

42.
The urban environment was to be read as a text

This suggests a readerly posture of detachment, like the contemporary academic who approaches texts vigilantly, ready to expose their ideological fault lines, assumptions, and omissions. That is rather distant, I think, from what the Lettrists and Situationists actually enacted with the *dérive*. Their meanders through the city were far more aimless and intoxicated. Literally intoxicated (they were often conducted in a state of inebriation), but also drunk in the sense of disoriented by the onrush of stimuli. The goal was to get lost, to lose command of oneself, through opening up to the random encounters and epiphanies that the city generated. The Lettrist artist Gil J. Wolman celebrated cities as "new, chaotic jungles, sparking experiences without purpose, devoid of meaning." Ivan Chtcheglov, who pioneered the concept of psychogeography in his *Formulary for a New Urbanism* (1958), recalled a period in 1953–1954 during which he and his associates "drifted for three or four months at a time: that's the extreme limit, the critical point. It's a miracle that it didn't kill us." Chtcheglov didn't mean physically kill, through exhaustion; he's talking here of a mental collapse, an unraveling of the psyche. "The continuous *dérive* is dangerous to the extent that the individual, having gone too far without defenses, is threatened with explosion, dissolution, disassociation, disintegration. And so the relapse into what is termed 'ordinary life,' which is to say, in reality, 'petrified life.'"

Especially in its double English meaning of frozen and fearful, "petrified" is a negative redescription of stability: life as a productive member of society, whose duties include not simply working but also consuming (what makes the economy go round), is seen as a form of living death. An "ordinary" transit across the city involves an expedition for the purposes of work or education, shopping or entertainment – and maybe, every few years or so, to vote. Routes that are literally routine. Drifting – like its more manic and collective cousin, the riot – is a carnivalesque overturning of this mundane cartography; the citizen-consumer's life is re-enchanted, turned into pure play. But where the riot is carnivalesque and Dionysian, the drift is dreamlike, a sleepwalk through the city. Like dreams, the *dérive* charges the environment with affect, but it is not about making the city legible, a text to be deciphered and understood. Perhaps, like a dream, there is a sensation of intense significance, but the meaning remains elusive. [SR]

43.
The city and the wanderer as a dialogue

In recent years the use of facial recognition software by law enforcement agencies has become more widespread and problematic across the globe. The relationship between the city and the wanderer is increasingly fractured by technology and its deployment. The para-architectures of enforcement and technology have begun to dictate who may wander the city and who may not, what is observed and what might be overlooked.

The combination of closed-circuit television (CCTV) and facial recognition software is a low-cost method of street surveillance, and is therefore considered a powerful policing tool, yet it is one with an inherent bias and, in many cities, a lack of legal clarity around its use. The use of closed-circuit surveillance image capture has prompted the contemporary law enforcement model known as "preemptive," "proactive," or "predictive" policing. This approach to policing involves the use of CCTV linked to large databases (including those of immigration, motor vehicle registration, and passport agencies) and enables images to be quickly matched to faces on the street.

The automation of basic policing duties proves problematic when this software has established inaccuracies identifying black, brown and Asian faces. This shortcoming is evidenced when scripts assume identities and create inaccurate virtual lineups for a perceived crime. The software is widely available: Amazon's off-the-shelf, cloud-based Rekognition software has been adopted across many government agencies in the United States, including the police in Orlando, Florida. At the time of writing, in response to the Black Lives Matter movement, Amazon has placed a one-year moratorium on police use of this platform due to concerns surrounding its use. Similarly, IBM has now stopped selling its general-purpose facial recognition software, citing its role in mass surveillance. The companies providing this software are retrospectively acknowledging the inbuilt prejudices of the platforms that have become intertwined with institutions of power.

In Australia, preemptive policing has been shown to disproportionately target young Aboriginal people and other people of color. Its use in the state of New South Wales (NSW) has been the subject of scrutiny, particularly NSW Police's Suspect Targeting Management Plan (STMP), a program concerned with the problem of reoffending. The plan profiles current offenders and people that police believe are likely to offend. To unpack this, this is a model that tries to guess who might commit a crime that has not yet been committed. To some of us, this may be a puzzling provocation, but to others it is a terrifying daily reality, whereby your activity in the world is mapped and tracked. Developed in 1999 by an intelligence section of NSW Police, the plan refers to the use of particular algorithms and risk assessment tools used by police to profile individuals into categories of offender (high-risk, medium-risk, and "sleeper"). This approach ostensibly enables police to better identify who may offend and who may reoffend. The algorithms are not publicly available, but a study by V. Sentas and C. Pandolfini has shown that, in 2015, across ten NSW local area commands, of persons targeted under the plan, 44.1% were identified as Aboriginal, 5.6% were identified as Middle Eastern, and 12.5% were identified as being of a Maori, Pacific Islander, African, Mediterranean, Indian, Sri Lankan, Eastern European, or East Asian background. Enacting this plan means that, with "reasonable suspicion," an officer may stop, search, or detain a person of interest. In 2014–2015 the youngest person targeted was just ten years old.

These and other models of preemptive policing go directly against notions of the city and the wanderer. In Australia, so-called "move-on" powers were adopted in the 1990s, which have prevented the gathering in and wandering of cities for some years – these powers enable police officers to question those moving through the city without clear purpose, and to direct persons or groups to move away from an area or to cease any particular conduct. The city isn't impartial, and one's freedom may be significantly compromised if an algorithm says so. [MP/BH]

44.
The city as a text to be (close-)read

In her essay "Digging Through Kathy Acker's Stuff," writer Dodie Bellamy, together with her partner Kevin Killian and Matias Viegener, executor of Kathy Acker's estate, try to figure out the text on one of Acker's dresses – a sheer black mesh Gaultier dress. The black gothic text on sheer black mesh is difficult to decipher and, after half an hour, Kevin Killian comes up with "too fab to." "[...] but then we gave up. I get a couple sheets of typing paper and slip them inside the dress, so that the goth text now lies on a white background. It is only then that I realize there are words arching beneath the cross as well. Too fab to – too fab to what?" [quote: Dodie Bellamy, *When the Sick Rule the World* (South Pasadena, CA: Semiotext(e), 2015) 144.] [LL]

45.
No, I walk...
I mostly walk

[SM]

Footnotes

46.
And to drift is to study

a,
Helen Harper Marquis, wearing a dress made from issues of the local newspaper *Vidette* in Pond Creek, Oklahoma. Forcing another reading of women's clothes. May 19, 1898.

b,
Ladies in customized newspaper costumes promoting *Le Soleil* and *Le Petit Sou*. The female attire of Crieuses and Banner Ladies becomes their capital. Read the news costume, the poster dress, crying apron, and tweeting hat! Early 20th century.

c,
Newspaperwomen and -men assembled to distribute an edition of *Le Matin*. In 1914 the newspaper sold more than a million copies a day. In 1930 *Paris-Soir* would sell up to two and a half million copies a day. A small army wearing self-made newspaper hats are the walking news tickers, systematically distributing the news through the streets. Paris, 1914.

d,
Newspaper seller presenting an ever-changing news screen. Berlin, ca. 1915.

e,
Suffragette Vera Wentworth campaigning for the enfranchisement of women. London, 1908.

Mabel Capper and Patricia Woodlock wearing newssheets as aprons, advertising a meeting in Heaton Park, Manchester, 1908.

They are the advance guard of the new womanhood. The Suffragette has come to stay.
– *The Suffragette*, November 18, 1912.

Suffrage worker with newspaper clippings on the passage of the Nineteenth Amendment, granting women the right to vote, by the U.S. Senate, 1919.

The suffragettes dressed to perfection, fashionable and elegant. Over and over, they marched the headlines of an anticipated future.

Women campaigning to vote on equal terms with men. London, 1927.

Footnotes

f,
Dressed up in a selection of international newspapers. Nice, France, January 1, 1925.

g,
Abstracted, activist, covered with slogans and statistics. The Soviet Woman by El Lissitzky and Mikhail Plaksin at the Soviet pavilion, Pressa, in Cologne, Germany, 1928.

The spectacular presentation was referred to as a drama that unfolds in time and space. Over five million visitors from all over the world came to see the exhibition.

h,
On a trip to Copenhagen, fashion designer Elsa Schiaparelli was struck by the queerly shaped paper hats of the women selling fish on the quay. After she returned to Paris, she reproduced a collage of her own newspaper reviews on fabric, from which she made “blouses, scarves, hats and all kinds of bathing nonsense.” Copenhagen, Denmark, 1930s.

A CHEERFUL GOOD-BYE.—A picture of Mrs. Mollison just before she set off this morning. Her smile indicates that she is not worrying unduly about what may happen.

i,
A scarf was added to the collection of clothes she designed for aviatrix Amy Johnson, turning her into a voluntarily newsgirl, distributing Elsa's old news. London, 1936. Photo by Sasha.

Amy Johnson was about to set a new record flying from Gravesend, England, to Cape Town, South Africa. Amy, as she stepped into the plane immediately before setting off, on the front page of the *Daily Mail*, April 3, 1936.

j,
The first bikini ever was printed with news, anticipating the impact it caused in the press, just as the nuclear tests on Bikini Atoll had four days earlier. Micheline Bernardini holds a cube capable of carrying the entire outfit.
Molitor Swimming Pool, Paris, July 5, 1946.

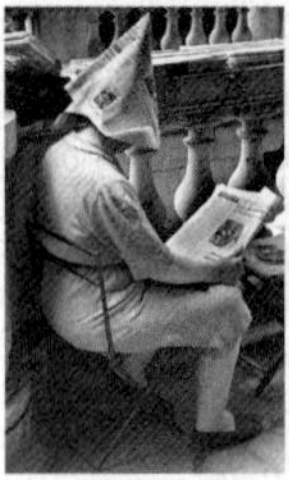

k,
Newsprint is cheap, impermanent, and brittle. Newswomen: Paris, 1947. Photo by Ilse Bing (left). Germany, 1952 (right).

Footnotes

l,
Behind the news, making the private public or vice versa? Audience at the Davis Cup Challenge Championship, Australia, 1963.

m,
After Greta Garbo retired from the screen, she wanted to be left alone. While she sought solitude and privacy, she was in some ways even more popular and mythologized. She conceals her face while being chased by photographer Sal Traina on West 57th Street in Manhattan, New York, November 9, 1966.

n,
After Jean Seberg's death in 1979, the FBI acknowledged that its counterintelligence program COINTELPRO was intended to discredit her support of the black nationalist movement by planting rumors in the press. Newspaper girl Jean Seberg in *À bout de souffle* by Jean-Luc Godard, 1960.

o,
Was the film *Critique de la séparation* by Guy Debord in 1961 an immediate and critical response to *À bout de souffle*?

p,
The *Daily Express* dubbed her the "Face of 1966" and launched the successful modeling career of "Twiggy (who) bends to every shape in fashion." Marshall McLuhan once stated, "Twiggy is an X-ray, not a picture." Twiggy in a dress with a print from the *Daily Express*, London, 1967.

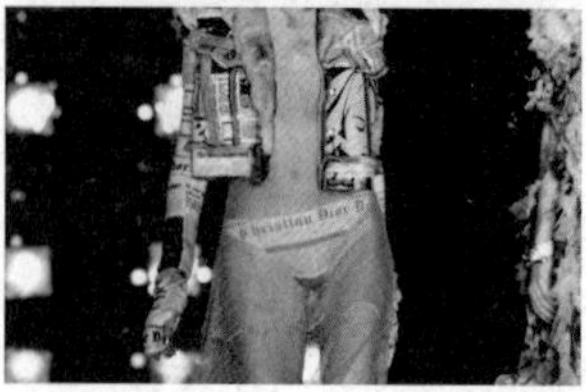

q,
John Galliano first used newspaper print in a controversial couture collection for Dior, inspired by the homeless in Paris and the "rag balls" in the Twenties, where the rich would dress up as the poor in shredded couture dresses. The newsprint was a collage of fashion stories by Suzy Menkes in *The International Herald Tribune*. Photo by Nick Knight, 2000.

Galliano created the fictional *Christian Dior Daily* for the ready-to-wear collection. The print was made up of the bad reviews he had received earlier.

For his own brand, he created the *Galliano Gazette*. Both newsprints, persistent and popular, still appear on items from leather to chiffon. Backstage, John Galliano, Fall 2004.

Footnotes

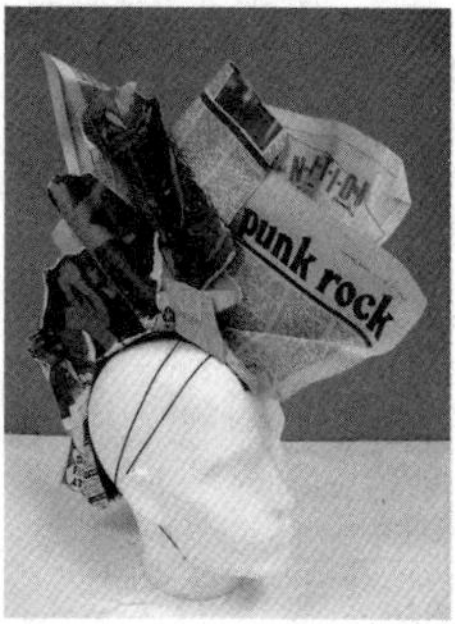

r,
Hat (fanzine) by British milliner Stephen Jones, 2006. The Met Collection, New York.

s,
As a special guest editor of the French newspaper *Libération*, Jean Paul Gauthier created 60 unique outfits made from old editions in which he and staff from the newspaper posed. The paper items seemed to refer to the origin of the *Libération*, which was founded in the wake of the protest movements of May 68, and celebrate the gestures of revolution, liberation, activism, and protest, as well as the anti-fashion statements of punk. June 14, 2011. Photos by Patrick Swirc.

t,
Meanwhile, protesters occupy Tahrir Square. Their paper hats read: “We are protesting this day, yesterday and the day before.” Tahrir Square, Cairo, February 18, 2011.

u,
A journalist shields herself with a newspaper outside the Mediclinic Heart Hospital in Pretoria, where president Nelson Mandela is hospitalized. June 2013. Photo by Eric Feferberg.

v,
Stella Tennant holds the bag as if it is a banner. The image is old news, summing it all up. As papers fade and news is questioned, newsprint persists in fashion. The news, an illegible collage in motion. Balenciaga campaign, Spring 2018.

w,
In 2018 the Museum of London acquired a look by New York fashion collective Vaquera. It is a remake of the dress and apron worn by suffragette Vera Wentworth in 1908. The original image has become a present past. Fashion's inimitable contribution to the politics of memory. June 2017.

x, y, z.
The catwalk has become the street we walk each season. The stage of Dior women's Fall/Winter collection was surfaced with a remade, pixelized edition of France's *Le Monde* newspaper: *Newsfloor (Le Monde Pixelisé)* by the collective Claire Fontaine. Paris, 2020.

[LD]

47.
And to drift is to study

See also Walter Benjamin's 1928 book, *One-Way Street*, and related essays collected as *One-Way Street and Other Writings* (London: Verso, 1979), as well as filmmaker Jem Cohen's Benjaminian trilogy of New York City films, *This is a History of New York* (1987), *Lost Book Found* (1996), and *Little Flags* (2000). [MO]

48.
And to drift is to study

If we are to treat the city like a language, or even as language, we must then also be willing to pose the question: who speaks? For the Situationists, it could only be capital itself. The city we wander through is the spatial mirror of those relations of exchange and exploitation, of commodity fetishism and uneven development, which at one and the same time actively shape and themselves are shaped by urban form. Techniques like *dérive* were attempts to make this landscape speak otherly and, in this sense, do indeed belong in a long genealogy of urban counter-practices going back to Baudelaire. But the Situationists' discursive politics of the city, like those of their predecessors, certainly had blind spots: their critical voice is an insistently masculine one, the voice of the "cowboy philosopher," as Greil Marcus incisively phrased it, who theorizes reification as he intrepidly wanders through the alienated streets. Kozintsev and Trauberg could imagine a young woman, the shop girl Louise Poirier (played by the amazing Yelena Kuzmina), at the heart of their tale of the Commune, but 30 years later women in the Situationist International were largely reduced to mute companions of the movement's male protagonists. How do women speak the city, how do they read its language? For that, we would have to turn away from the Situationists and ask Florence "Cléo" Victoire, or Juliette Jeanson, or Jeanne Dielman, among many possible voices. [TM]

49.
And to drift is to study

Bernstein's two novels are, in my view, underrated as sources of Situationist thinking. They are all too often just mined for biographical hints about Debord. Her second book, *The Night*, is one of the best accounts of a *dérive* that we have. I've walked much of it myself, and it's a magnificent journey through the ambiences of even today's Paris. In that book, she reimagines the form of the novel in which the *dérive* could be central and writes her way out of private property, both in terms of imagining the space of the city but also those of intimate relationships. On top of that, it's a *détournement* of the "new novel" that was all the rage at the time. [MW]

50.
And to drift is to study

It's easy to conflate Debord's drifter with the figure of the *flâneur*. Both present similar affectations: Charles Baudelaire's observer strolled the boulevards of modern urban life with detachment, while the Situationist *dérive* encouraged a mannered disorientation as one pinballed across Paris. Yet I've always interpreted the drifter as a gumshoe – a private investigator gathering urban clues. This understanding, as well as any understanding about how to literally read the city, may come from reading Paul Auster's *City of Glass*. There's a mystery novel embedded in the 1985 novel, or maybe it's the other way around. Either way, authors, writers, protagonists, and detectives become intertwined. Even the city. "By wandering aimlessly, all places became equal, and it no longer mattered where he was," writes Auster. And the city, too, is both character and text. The wanderings of one character – up, down, and around city blocks – resolves into the letter form E, then R. Or maybe O. Cartographies that, combined with the charting of other seeming drifts, turn streets into alphabets. [MZ]

51.
Walls and words

What did the walls of Paris actually look like? One source are the "décollages" of the artist group Les Affichistes, who roamed the city in search of densely layered and lacerated posters to tear down, trim, and exhibit. Its members were three: Jacques Villeglé and Raymond Hains, acquaintances of the Lettrist International, who evolved the practice in 1949, and François Dufrêne, a founding member of the LI, who joined the Affichistes at around the time the LI dissolved into the Situationist International.

A history of French graphic design and its messages could be written through their work, but also its antidote: the small acts of rebellion committed against the dominant monologue every time an anonymous pedestrian ripped into the graphic surface of the streets. [LW]

52.
That typical Situationist method of visual appropriation

Asger Jorn's visual language worked on an abstract level, of which the diagram of the city could be just one example. It was scale free and could apply anywhere. *The Situationist Times*, edited by Jacqueline de Jong, explored and expanded on the topologies of the ring, the knot, and so on. It was a revolutionary project to do away with the constricting diagrams of form inherited from the classical world of Greece and Rome. [MW]

53.
Use of diagrams

The Black Archives is an Amsterdam-based cultural center and archive focusing on black history, art, culture, and literature. The library collection is organized by category, each marked – at least when I visited the archive in April 2019 – with provisional, handwritten labels, taped to the shelf. The label "gender" has a double-headed arrow next to it, signifying that the category is spread out over top and bottom shelves. At the same time, it may also be read as a provisional sign for gender equality. [LL]

54.
Map of Paris

I don't think "Naked City" and the various other maps Debord made, with or without Jorn, are meant just to be metaphors. Some are actual experimental research on the psychogeography of the city. I have walked a fair bit of this map and it actually works, even taking in to account the changes in Paris since it was made. One cannot be a Situationist without doing the legwork. [MW]

55.
Map of Paris

The map cut up by Debord and Jorn to make theirs – the *Plan de Paris à vol d'oiseau* – was the dominant guide to the topography of Paris for most of the 20th century. Like all conventional maps, it pretends to be absolute, though it is essentially ephemeral and limited, because cities are always changing. Debord and Jorn could have made "The Naked City" a dozen times over and never been done with it. Indeed, the SI were continually mapping and remapping the city of Paris, because they were concerned with how the city felt to real people, rather than the way it was organized by official planners.

The Plan de Paris has continued to be ripe for artistic appropriation. In 2003 the Palais de Tokyo published a series of altered *Plans* as affordable multiples, including Franck Scurti's *Topo-Typographie*. Scurti identified existing street configurations that traced each of the 26 letters of the alphabet, suggesting all kinds of possible connections between the city and language, walking, and writing. [LW]

56.
Printed matter and the city

In his novel *Notre Dame de Paris* (1831), Victor Hugo famously put language against architecture. The book and the printing press were to kill architecture as a discipline of communication and collective meaning. Language and the art of printing are like a virus overcoming the stone and steel structures.

Is this a parasitic, metabolic relation? Like the Darwinian wasps who use living caterpillars as host bodies for their eggs and larvae? Or could it be more symbiotic? As suggested by Deleuze and Guattari: the orchid attracting the wasp by becoming wasp-like and vice versa. Different acts of appropriation, and of metamorphosizing. [DH]

57.
Printed matter and the city

Debord borrowed the name for his map from an American film noir, *The Naked City*, directed by Jules Dassin and released in 1948. Perhaps Debord saw it as a teenager while still in the south of France, or maybe he watched it as a cinephilic twenty-something after his move to Paris. In either case, he must have been drawn to the film's psychogeographic attention to the city as not just a setting for its action but a veritable character in itself, and to its synoptic overview of Manhattan's social diversity, ranging from aeries of the wealthy to tenement slums. What was *dérive* if not a similar, quasi-anthropological crossing of the city's social boundaries? And just as the film's detectives sought to assemble disparate clues into a convincing narrative of a crime – tellingly, the murder of a beautiful young woman in her bathtub – so Debord and his colleagues were seeking to stitch together the suggestions that certain neighborhoods, certain streets, offered of a different city, a different life. Behind the veil of the everyday, the map suggested, lay passion, quest, adventure. In France, *The Naked City* was released as *La cité sans voiles*, or "The City Unveiled." Stripped bare, we could say, in another gendered metaphor. But isn't Debord's map itself a kind of veil, a modest sheet of paper that, by overlaying the city's built form with an alternative cartographic language, seeks to remake its subject? *Ceci tuera cela*, Victor Hugo wrote a decade before Marx's injunction to "humanize the circumstances" of our existence – "this will kill that," the printed book will kill the building, or, in the parlance of an American children's game, "paper covers rock." At its heart, Hugo was speaking of textual egalitarianism as opposed to architectural hierarchy (the Greek *arkhi-*, after all, meant "chief").
To humanize the city is to write it anew, the meandering line of *dérive* weaving another possible form of urban life. [TM]

58.
Provo was an anarchist movement that existed for just two years (1965–1967)

In fact – just before Provo, there was *Barst*.

In April 1965, and under the moniker of the Anarchistische Werkgroep Zaanstreek, a nineteen-year-old Rob Stolk (who, only a few weeks later, would become one of the main founders of the Provo movement), released the first (and only) issue of the anarchist magazine *Barst* (which can be translated as either "Crack" or "Burst").

Designed and published by Rob Stolk, the editorial team of *Barst* consisted of Rob, Sara Duys, Garmt Kroeze, and Klaas de Vries. The magazine featured contributions by people such as Roel van Duijn and Hans Tuynman, while the illustrations, as well as the front and back covers, were created by Rob's brother, Swip Stolk (under the pseudonym ZAS).

The specific binding of *Barst* was quite inventive – folded as an A5-sized booklet, the publication unwraps into a stapled A4-sized zine. An accompanying letterhead was produced as well.

In *Imaazje: De Verbeelding van Provo, 1965–1967* (Wereldbibliotheek, 2003), Niek Pas notes that, for the mimeographic reproduction of *Barst*, Rob received technical help from both *De Vrije* (the Netherlands' oldest anarcho-socialist magazine, founded in 1898 by Domela Nieuwenhuis), and from a befriended member of the PSP (the Dutch Pacifist-Socialist Party).

In other words, *Barst* is a good example of the way in which the Provo movement was ultimately rooted in a much older revolutionary Dutch tradition – a graphic tradition, to be specific.

What's also interesting to mention is the linguistic link between *Barst* ("Crack"), and the Dutch word for squatting, "kraken" ("to crack open"). In fact, it was Rob Stolk who coined the verb "kraken" (in the specific sense of "to squat a house"), when he founded Woningburo De Kraker back in 1968 (three years after *Barst*).

In our view, there's an interesting line to be drawn from pre-Provo *barsten* to post-Provo *kraken* – an ongoing search for the cracks in the law, the cracks in society, and the cracks in reality. [EJ]

59.
The Netherlands and abroad

In the late 1960s many artists moved outdoors, showing their work in the city and on the street. This brought a new artistic freedom, and with it, other opportunities. The audience changed from passive observer to active participant. The city, with its parks, squares, and pavements, played an important role in this.

In Amsterdam, Koert Stuyf replaced stone pavers with a springy variant, while Wim T. Schippers set up a Christmas tree in front of the American Hotel on Leidseplein in the middle of summer. In June 1967 the Eventstructure Research

Group, an international artists' collective including Theo Botschuyver and Jeffrey Shaw, performed their first trials with large inflatable tubes in Amsterdam's Flevopark.

The outcome was a series of inflatable structures with different shapes. These airy objects were allowed to be touched by everyone. They encouraged having fun.

In 1969 the Eventstructure Research Group staged "six events" at various locations in Amsterdam, from Museumplein to the Sloterplas. At the latter, a lake, anyone who felt like trying to walk on water, all the while falling and regaining their feet, could do so in a blow-up pyramid called *Waterwalk*.

Designer Iris de Leeuw, together with the collective Luuks Laboratorium, performed experiments focusing on the social space between people. She designed the androgynous "speespak" ("space suit") as a garment intended for a new era. It had a distinctive zipper that ran around the tops of both trouser legs, allowing the legs to be unzipped (preferably by another person). De Leeuw explained the idea behind the space suit as follows: "If you happen to meet someone wearing different 'Luuks trousers' – you can just swap them, of course (once given, no taking it back) – a great communicative activity in the street."

Other events in the streets of Amsterdam were more political in nature, like those of Dolle Mina, founded with the goal of exposing the socioeconomic inequality between men and women through very concrete actions. As of January 1970, the Dolle Minas ("Mad Minas") knew how to associate the playful with the political through unconventional actions and demonstrations, thereby drawing the attention of the press and public. The Amsterdam group purposefully used Provo tactics. Their actions were just as playful, funny, and unsettling, but were now being deployed for a clearly feminist purpose. For instance, during demonstrations for the legalization of abortion and use of the contraceptive pill, the Dolle Minas carried with them large white pills made of cardboard. In response to the lack of public toilets for women, the members of the "Double Sexual Morality" work group unveiled a huge papier-mâché phallus on Rembrandtplein that could be used as a toilet. As counterpart to the female nudity seen in the surrounding nightclubs, a male stripper came along to officially open the ladies' restroom. [LC]

60.
Conceptual activism and speculative political proposals

These *White Plans* seem to encapsulate the Provo

movement in a nutshell.
A collection of pamphlets and articles published between 1965 and 1967, the *White Plans* were basically a series of conceptual propositions, Presented as "white" (as in: open) gestures, these plans functioned as Fluxus-like interventions in the political landscape. Included in these plans were the *White Bicycle Plan*, *White Chimney Plan*, *White Wives Plan*, *White Chicken Plan*, *White Housing Plan*, *White Kids Plan*, *White Victim Plan*, *White Car Plan*, *White Sex Plan*, *White School Plan*, *White City Plan*, and *White Corps Plan*.

When Provo turned into a political party, many of these plans were incorporated in the official party program. Although many were never realized in the lifetime of Provo, echoes of them can be found in many social and "green" policies that we nowadays take for granted. The *White Bike Plan,* for example, has been the main inspiration behind many of today's "public bicycle" programs that flourish in major capitals around the world. [EJ]

61.
Auto-provocation

After Provo came to an end, Rob Stolk made a "Call to Permanent Revolution."

In this poster we see a typical Amsterdam house (split in a way that reminds us of the projects from the mid-seventies by Gordon Matta-Clark), with the words "Destruction is Construction" coming out. [LC]

62.
Auto-provocation

The liquidation of Provo was the movement's final masterpiece, a gesture that was in many ways more significant than the movement's foundation.

During the first months of 1967, a small group within Provo was already planning the movement's abolishment. In the view of this faction (later known as the "Provo Likwiedaatsie Kommissie"), the blown-up image of Provo had turned against the movement itself, and became counter-productive. In order for the individual Provos to be able to continue their activist agendas and subversive activities, the image ("imaazje") of Provo had to be dismantled in a final, auto-destructivist happening.

The famous poster (drawn, written, and printed by Rob Stolk) triggered this final event, announcing the liquidation that would take place on May 13, 1967, at the "spieker's corner" (speaker's corner) in the Vondelpark. By simply creating this poster and hanging it at a few Provo spots, the end of the movement was a fact. The power of print in full effect.

The poster literally shows the split within the "House of Provo," the drawing clearly depicting *Karthuizerstraat 14, Amsterdam* (the building that Roel van Duijn, Carla Kuit, Rob Stolk, and Sara Duijs shared together during the Provo years – Roel/Carla on the first floor and Rob/Sara on the second floor). It's not hard to imagine that the caricature of the bearded person, peeking through the window above the door, is in fact referring to Van Duijn.

Through our research, we discovered that the original layouts of issue 14 of *Provo* magazine (February 15, 1967) already contained a short open letter written by the pro-liquidation faction (signed by Rob Stolk and Lou/Loe van Nimwegen, together with an unidentified Anton), announcing their withdrawal from Provo.

This letter can be found in the so-called "paste-ups": the camera-ready artwork of the magazine, set to be reproduced. The note is even apparent in the transparent film negatives that were made from these paste-ups. However, in the eventual printed version of issue 14 of *Provo* magazine, the letter has disappeared.

Our own theory (which is pure speculation) is that Rob Stolk removed the letter from the printing plate, right before printing. He must have felt that the liquidation of Provo needed a more significant moment – and hence, he pulled the letter, and planned a bigger finale: the liquidation as took place on May 13, 1967.

There exists some footage of this final happening. The Dutch TV show *Monitor* (NTS, 1967) shows a tumultuous public meeting in which all speakers say exactly the opposite of what they mean. Arch-enemies (such as mayor Van Hall) are being described as best friends, Van Heutsz is elevated to an actual movement ("Van Heutszism"), and speakers worry openly about Provos now being unemployed, during an absurdist performance of irony and wordplay.

A couple of months after the self-liquidation of Provo at the Vondelpark, the Hippies repeated the gesture, at the Buena Vista Park in San Francisco (the notorious "Hippie Funeral" of October 6, 1967). [EJ]

63.
Woningburo De Kraker, 1968

Rob Stolk has actually been in prison twice – in 1968, for publishing the so-called "Subversive Letter," and in 1969, for his involvement in the occupation of Het Maagdenhuis (University of Amsterdam).

During his six-week prison stay in 1968, Rob found himself surrounded by people who referred to themselves as "kluiskrakers" and "autokrakers" – safe crackers and car jackers.

That's when he got the idea of referring to the act of squatting as "kraken" – literally, the act of "cracking open" a house. The time in prison also gave Rob time to think about the legal loopholes that made squatting possible in the first place.

Immediately after his release, he ran into a friend and enthusiastically told him about his plans to start an action committee solely dedicated to squatting: Woningburo De Kraker.

Woningburo De Kraker ("The Squatter Housing Agency") consisted of Rob and a couple of his close friends (including Tjebbe van Tijen and Tom Bouman), and had as its slogan "Woningburo De Kraker doet het steeds vaker" – "The Squatter Housing Agency does it again and again."

Shortly after the founding of Woningburo De Kraker, they published their notorious "Krakershandleiding" (or "Handleiding Krakers") – an A4-sized, fourteen-page squatters' manual (consisting of instructions, statements, articles, and newspaper clippings), featuring a brightly screen-printed cover.

What's particularly interesting about this cover is the inclusion of the slogan "Redt un pandje, bezet un pandje" ("Save a space, occupy a space"), as it clearly illustrates the direct link between the Provo movement (which liquidated itself in 1967), and the organized squatting movement (which emerged in 1968). After all, "Redt un pandje, bezet un pandje" was a typical Provo slogan, and already appeared in pamphlets such as the *Witte Huizenplan* (*White Housing Plan*) from 1966.

Another direct link can be found in the financing of the manual. The publication (as well as other activities related to Woningburo De Kraker and Aktiegroep Nieuwmarkt) was funded by the Dadaistically named "Stichting ter Bevordering van een Goed en Goedkoop Leven," which was basically the money that Rob (and some of his close allies) received from selling his personal Provo archive to the University of Amsterdam (UvA), immediately after the liquidation of Provo (this money was mainly used for paying off some old debts made by the Provo movement, as well as supporting various post-Provo action groups).

The fact that this Provo archive provided the economic underpinnings of so many post-Provo activities (most of them related to squatting, and the Nieuwmarkt protests) is a wonderfully concrete example of the way in which activism and archivism constantly influence each other in order to enable each other.

Yet another illustration of the direct lineage between the Provo movement and the early squatting subculture can be found in the "Krakersfilm" ("Squatters' Movie"), a nine-minute fragment of a never-completed documentary from 1969, produced by Pieter Boersma (photography), Robert Hartzema (editing), and Otto Schuurman (cinematography), chronicling the early squatters' scene in the Dappermarkt and Nieuwmarkt areas. The documentary features a group of activists (including Ad Leeflang, Tjebbe van Tijen, Rob Stolk, and Pieter Boersma, among others) occupying some abandoned houses at the Wijttenbachstraat.

Again, what is particularly interesting about this footage is the direct link being made with Provo. The documentary starts with an image of a Provo pamphlet from 1966, announcing the *White Housing Plan*. Meanwhile, a voice-over proclaims the text of the pamphlet, including slogans that are typical for Provo ("Redt un pandje, bezet un pandje," "Lieverevolutie," etc.), while other phrases being used in the film ("Gnot Tempel," "Magies Sentrum," and "Imaazje") stem directly from the vocabulary of Robert Jasper Grootveld. In other words – it's a movie that clearly documents the transitional period from Provo to the early squatters' scene, and it's too bad it was never completed (let alone distributed). [EJ]

64.
Aktiegroep Nieuwmarkt

In fact, it might be more appropriate to speak of "Aktiegroepen Nieuwmarkt" – in plural.

Aktiegroepen Nieuwmarkt was the loose-knitted collective of action committees that, between 1967 and 1976, were united in their combined struggle against the city council's plans to demolish the Nieuwmarkt area, as well as other parts of the city De Jordaan, De Pijp), to make way for office buildings, highways, and subway stations.

Affiliated magazines were *Lastage*, *Bethaniënnieuws*, *Nieuwsmarkt*, *Nieuwmarkt Weekblad/Dagblad*, *Amsterdams Weekblad*, and (later) *De Tand des Tijds*.

The history of this particular struggle has been captured in the great *De Beste Aktiegroep ter Wereld* (De Oude Stad, 1984). [EJ]

65.
Aktiegroep Nieuwmarkt

As a child in the mid-seventies, I grew up in Amsterdam close to the Nieuwmarkt area. And I remember the strong resistance by the local community against the demolition of the whole historical area to make way for the subway. At that time, I also witnessed the clashes between the people living the neighborhood and the police.

I recently found this *Nieuwmarkt Dagblad* from March 26, 1975, in my personal archive, a daily made by the Aktiegroep Nieuwmarkt.

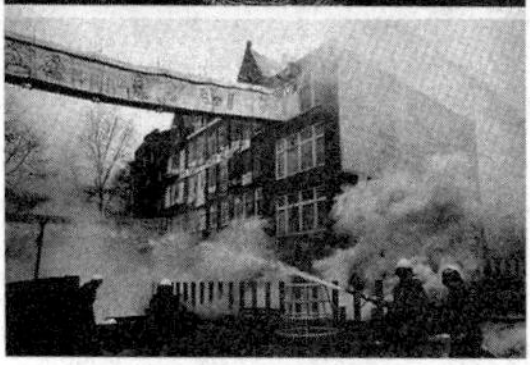

This newspaper contains personal stories about violent evictions by the police and information for students about housing shortage and squatting. The photographs testify to the violence of the police, who were armed with tear gas grenades, masks, and carbines, and used water cannons against the demonstrators. [LC]

66.
Magazines were distributed in the streets

During its short existence (1965–1967), the Provo movement published several magazines – first of all, there was *Provo*, the monthly journal around which the whole movement revolved. In total, fifteen issues appeared.

Other Provo-produced titles included the weekly *Image* and the ongoing series of pamphlets known as *Provokaties*. On top of that, the Provo movement also published *God, Nederland & Oranje*, a bimonthly zine dedicated to cartoons. In 1967 Provo also published two fake newspapers designed to closely mimic the tone and layout of *De Telegraaf* (The Telegraph), a Dutch right-wing populist newspaper. The Provos named their satirical newspaper *De Teleraaf* (The Teleraven), and filled it with absurdist news, taking *De Telegraaf*'s right-wing ideology and stretching it beyond its breaking point. [EJ]

67.
Performances ("happenings") took place on public squares and around specific statues

By staging site-specific performances (happenings, rituals, protest marches, etc.) around well-chosen statues, the city's public sculptures and monuments were transformed into archetypes within the larger Provo narrative. Each icon referred to well-known models within the pantheon of Provo – *Het Lieverdje* stood for the youngster, the nozem, the juvenile consumer, both innocent and corruptible; *De Dokwerker* represented the worker, the laborer, the old proletariat; the statue of Ferdinand Domela Nieuwenhuis symbolized Provo's anarcho-pacifist roots; while the Van Heutsz monument referred to the authoritarian figure, the powers that had to be defeated.

By remaking the statues of Amsterdam into Provotarian archetypes, Provo effectively turned the layout of the city into a symbolical, psychogeographical space – a platform for collective semiotic and linguistic action.

As it happens, the Dutch word "beeld" has two meanings: "statue" and "image." It seems only logical that Provo, a movement so dedicated to the notion of the "blown-up" image (both the *enlarged* image and the *deconstructed* image), had a particular interest in statues as well. It all comes down to the *détournement* of "beelden" – in both senses of the word. [EJ]

68.
Pamphlets

Just about any interview with bass player Mike Watt makes mention of the fact that his band The Minutemen (1980–1985) held strong to the dichotomy that everything is either "a flyer" or "a gig." "Flyer," signifying anything and everything (records, posters, fanzines, flyers) that would get the audience to "the gig." [LL]

69.
Protesters filled the roads with smoke signals

The most iconic use of these smoke signals took place on March 10, 1966. What happened on that specific day in Amsterdam is well-documented (see, for example, Niek Pas's excellent *Imaazje: De Verbeelding van Provo, 1965–1967*), and remains one of the most important dates in the short history of Provo.

We are obviously talking about the wedding procession of Crown Princess Beatrix and Prince Claus, which led to small riots when smoke "bombs" were being thrown by Provos and other protestors (in fact, "smoke screens" is a more fitting, less judgmental word).

A week after the wedding procession, a small exhibition was installed at the space of publisher Polak & Van Gennep. The exhibition (featuring photos by Cor Jaring, Ed van der Elsken, Koen Wessing, and G.J. Wolffensperger) documented the police brutality that took place during those protests of the 10th of March. Co-organized by Provo (in collaboration with local magazines *Propria Cures*, *Links*, and *Yang*), the show opened on March 19th with a legendary speech by the Dutch writer Jan Wolkers; an event famously filmed by Dutch avant-garde director Louis van Gasteren. While hundreds of people were waiting in the street to enter the gallery space, the police entered the scene again, launching an attack on the unsuspecting public.

In *Provo: Amsterdam's Anarchist Revolt* (Autonomedia, 2007), Richard Kempton quotes Roel van Duijn describing the whole event as a "spiegelbeeld-provokatie" ("mirrored provocation"): people inside the gallery, looking at pictures of police brutality, while actual police brutality was going on outside the gallery. Director Louis van Gasteren and cinematographer Theo Hogers perfectly captured this situation in "Omdat Mijn Fiets Daar Stond" ("Because My Bike Stood There"), a hallucinatory mixture of experimental cinema and propaganda tactics. After the opening speech by Jan Wolkers, the short movie focuses (in graphic repetition) on one of the victims of the police attack.

Of particular interest is the manner in which Jan Wolkers discusses the "smoke bombs" that were being used by the protesters on March 10 (and technically speaking, these weren't really "bombs," but non-explosive devices produced to create smoke screens).

Wolkers indeed refers to these screens as "smoke signals, one of the oldest languages in the world," which is a great way to describe the way in which the Provo movement managed to use the city as a platform to showcase these smoke signals – as a ludic stage for this archetypical form of communication. It perfectly encapsulates the Provotarian interpretation of Amsterdam – the city as a device to produce and reproduce language. [EJ]

70.
White bikes

The Provo bicycle-sharing scheme inspired one of the most exciting singles of the

Sixties: "My White Bicycle" by Tomorrow, who alongside Pink Floyd and Soft Machine were staples of London's leading psychedelic club UFO. When LSD and Indian raga guitar transformed the sound of British beat music, the band dropped their original, Mod-era moniker, the In-Crowd, for the appropriately utopian and forward-looking new name, Tomorrow. They also changed their image, adopting the psychedelic dandy look then emerging at trendy boutiques like Granny Takes A Trip. According to Tomorrow's drummer, Twink, it was actually the co-owner of Granny Takes A Trip, Nigel Weymouth, who hipped them to what was going on in Amsterdam. "Nigel had gone there and come back with a Provos badge which he gave to me. They were kind of a student anarchist group that believed everything should be free. In fact, they had white bicycles in Amsterdam and they used to leave them around the town. And if you were going somewhere and you needed to use a bike, you'd just take the bike and you'd go somewhere and just leave it. Whoever needed the bikes would take them and leave them around when they were done."

The song conveys the freewheeling exhilaration of riding a bicycle through the city at the dead of night ("four o'clock and they're all asleep"), most likely under the influence of mind-altering substances. The protagonist knocks over dustbins, is unbothered by the pelting rain. One of the most thrilling moments comes when a police constable hollers at him to stop, but the youth hurtles on regardless: "Policeman shouts but I don't see him / They're one thing I don't believe in."

Tomorrow's guitarist was Steve Howe, later of the progressive rock giants Yes. Prog was the prime target of punk, and regarded as its aesthetic and political antithesis: elitist, out of touch, overblown, ripe to be overthrown. Yet Keith Levene, a founding member of the Clash and then the musical mainstay of Public Image Ltd (Johnny Rotten's post-punk initiative after leaving the Sex Pistols), was a huge fan of Howe, and even briefly worked as a teenage roadie for Yes. Levene would disguise and mutilate the Howe influence in his playing for PiL, incorporating wrong notes and discordance but not completely concealing his own hard-earned virtuosity on the instrument.

The line in "My White Bicycle" about not believing in the police shows a deep continuity of spirit – beneath the superficial style differences – that connects the blissed-out and play-powered anarchism of 1967 and the more wanton and chaotic anarchism of 1977. From Tomorrow to "no future," from Yes to "no," punk is the second act of a play whose first act unfolded in the Sixties. [SR]

71.
Applied utopianism

Work is play
Love is play
Memory is play
Peace is play
Pray is play
Duty is play
Ego is play
Respect is play
Revoluion is play
Rain is play
Rain is play
Japan is play
1917 is play
Belief is play
Doubt is play
Croissant is play
Pasta is play
House is play
Family is play
City is play
Dopamine is play
Scorpion is play
Scorpion is play
Scorpion is play
Woman is play
Man is play
You are play
I am play

PlayPlayPlayPlayPlayPlayPlay
PlayPlayPlayPlayPlayPlay
PlayPlayPlayPlayPlay
PlayPlayPlayPlay
PlayPlayPlay
PlayPlay
Play
[SM]

72.
The printing press

Indeed – as the Provos were drifting through the city, and as this *dérive* continued throughout the post-Provo period, the location of the printing press constantly shifted. But not only the location changed – the method of printing transformed as well: from mimeography to screen print, and from screen print to offset. In that sense, each printing technique corresponded with a specific area in the city. In other words, there's an interesting correlation between method and space to be found here. The printing press colored the city, as the city colored the printing press. [EJ]

73.
Provo turned the city into a place where ideas were enlarged, multiplied, and reproduced...

...and let's not forget – archived.

Researching the Provo movement, and its post-Provo offshoots, it is impossible not to be struck by the symbiotic relationship between the archivist and the activist – two roles that are fully dependent on each other. Activism generates archives, archives generate activism – and so forth.

Let's not forget that Provo, a movement that might appear to some people as phenomenon without history, was in fact very much inspired by the early socialist, anarchist, and pacifist movements that existed in the Netherlands between the

First and Second World Wars (decades before the birth of Provo).

In Niek Pas' *Imaazje: De Verbeelding van Provo, 1965–1967* (Wereldbibliotheek, 2003), there is a wonderful paragraph in which Rob Stolk recalls that, during his childhood years, he was very impressed by the bookshelves of Van der Veen, the father of a friend. Through these shelves, Rob came across revolutionary thinkers such as Domela Nieuwenhuis (1846–1919), whose ideas would become very influential to Provo. In other words, it was book collections, libraries, and archives that served as some of Provo's biggest inspirations.

And all throughout the actions of Provo, the archive continued to play an important role. Already during its existence, Provo actively documented itself – magazine articles were saved, photos were collected, scrapbooks were compiled.

During some of the Provo happenings that took place around *Het Lieverdje* (the statue at Spui Square), a large cardboard folder was carried around, adorned with a brick wall pattern. This folder contained a large collection of newspaper clippings, all on the subject of Provo. The role of this cardboard folder was almost ritual – it was placed against the statue, people dancing around it frantically, bearing torches and slogans. Seen that way, the archive became the heart of the happening, the center of the movement itself. The archive was transformed into a battery, an accumulator, a generator of activism.

A very concrete example of this (activism being generated by the archive) took place during the final stages of Provo. Immediately after the 1967 liquidation (or better said, self-liquidation) of Provo, Rob Stolk and a couple of his close friends decided to sell their personal Provo material to the library of the University of Amsterdam (UvA). This act (the selling of the archive) was certainly meant as a conceptual, artistic gesture: as the "final provocation." A special committee was invented (the "Provo Likwiedaatsie Kommissie"), and managed (after bluffing that an American university was interested in buying the archive) to make a deal with the University of Amsterdam – in total, a sum of 13,010 guilders was paid for the archive.

The transfer of this archive was actually captured on film. The movie (quite proto-punk in its conception – part *Great Rock & Roll Swindle*, part *Great Train Robbery*) shows Rob and his friends, dressed as gangsters, driving around in Amsterdam while carrying plastic machine guns and a large trunk filled with archival material. After the trunk was delivered at the university, the Provos (still dressed as mobsters, and carrying toy guns) went to the bank to deposit the money – where they were immediately arrested by police officers who thought they stumbled onto an actual bank robbery.

Adding even more to the conceptual, ludic (and self-mythologizing) nature of the transaction was the list of absurdist conditions stated by the Provo Likwiedaatsie Kommissie. For the next five years, none of the material was allowed to be reproduced – while for a period of 25 years the correspondence (the part of the archive that was gifted rather than sold) could only be visited with strict permission of the Kommissie. At the same time, all members of the Kommissie (Rob Stolk, Loe/Lou van Nimwegen, Robert Jasper Grootveld, and Steef Davidson) had unlimited access to the archive.

In Derek Taylor's *It Was Twenty Years Ago Today* (Bantam Press, 1987), Rob describes the transaction as follows:

In fact it wasn't an archive at all, just some scattered documentation, if you want to call it that. We spread a rumour via some journalist that the Provo archive would be sold to an American university, so the University of Amsterdam decided to buy the archive itself. They paid 13,010 guilders for it, at that time a huge amount of money, and then they started a real archive. A lot of people were interested in the movement but heard about it only when Provo was already dead so for us it was really useful – we could say "Go and read about it!" [...] Now the University has a big department with all kinds of material and publications of those times, from any country in the world where something was happening. So now there is a big archive.

From the 13,010 guilders that the Provo Likwiedaatsie Kommissie received from the University of Amsterdam, 3,000 guilders were donated to Robert Jasper Grootveld, and his Lowland Weed Company. The rest of the money (10,000 guilders) was used to found (and fund) the Stichting ter Bevordering van een Goed en Goedkoop Leven ("Foundation for the Promotion of Good and Cheap Living"), an action committee that played a crucial role in both the early squatters' movement (Woningburo De Kraker) and Aktiegroep Nieuwmarkt (the resistance against the total demolition of the Amsterdam's Nieuwmarkt area).

In other words, it was the death of Provo (and the act of selling of the archive) that enabled these new movements to take place – like a Provotarian phoenix rising from its ashes. A very clear illustration of activism being generated by an archive that was generated by activism.

The Provo archive remained in the library of the University in Amsterdam until 1990 (carefully maintained by people like archivist-activist-artist Tjebbe van Tijen), when it was transferred to the International Institute of Social History (IISG), where it is currently accessible to the public – and hopefully functions as a new generator for both activism and archivism. [EJ]

74.
The symbol of the apple

The sign was presented during "Open het Graf" ("Open the Tomb"), a legendary happening that took place on December 9, 1962, at Gallery Rik van Benum, situated on Prinsengracht 146. Co-organized by beat poet Simon Vinkenoog (who played an important role in many Dutch postwar subcultures and movements), "Open het Graf" is widely regarded as the first "real" happening to take place in the Netherlands.

As for the word "Gnot" – this was yet another Grootveldian invention, a neologism mainly referring to the Dutch word "genot" (joy), although associations with terms such as "god" and "gnost" (gnosis) were certainly intentional. (In previous texts we wrote on Provo, we sometimes tried to translate the word "Gnot" as "Njoy" – a pretty insufficient translation, as it certainly doesn't cover the full spectrum of possible meanings.) [EJ]

75.
Magies Sentrum (Magick Center)

The first time we heard Robert Jasper Grootveld speak about Amsterdam as the "Magick Center" was during the opening of an exhibition by Wolf Vostell at Galerie Monet, on Rokin in Amsterdam, on October 5, 1962. Vostell had invited several Fluxus artists, among which Nam June Paik, Alison Knowles, LaMonte Young, Emmett Williams, Willem de Ridder, and Dick Higgins, to perform their compositions. These events took place not only in the gallery but also in front of the building on the busy street. Many passers-by – unknowingly – became part of the performances. After the happenings in front of the gallery had finished, the program continued in the streets of Amsterdam. It was announced that Nam June Paik's *Moving Theater No. 1* would start at 10 p.m. with a walk to the Stedelijk Museum, accompanied by music. During their tour through the streets of Amsterdam, Tibetan songs were sung and actions were performed by Paik, Williams, Higgins, and others. [LC]

76.
Magies Sentrum (Magick Center)

In Eric van Duivenvoorden's *Magiër van de Nieuwe Tijd: Het Leven van Robert Jasper Grootveld* (De Arbeiderspers, 2009), Robert Jasper Grootveld remembers how the idea of Amsterdam as "Magies Sentrum" ("Magick Center") came to him, in 1962 – almost like a vision. "I had a dream that night – I dreamed that Amsterdam became the center of the Western asphalt jungle, the magic center." Grootveld imagined thousands of American beatniks and hippies, coming to Amsterdam – a vision that became reality just a couple of years later. [EJ]

77.
Magies Sentrum (Magick Center)

Let's acknowledge how problematic this idea is. Amsterdam is perhaps the prototype of a modern, strictly capitalist, imperial city whose mission is the exploitation of the world. We need a postcolonial spatial imaginary. To offer just one counter-imaginary, let's take the mythology of the Detroit techno duo Drexciya, who imagine their sound coming from an underwater Atlantis built by the mutant descendants of the pregnant slaves thrown overboard as valueless during the Middle Passage. [MW]

78.
Brick wall pattern

You say to a brick, "What do you want, brick?" And brick says to you, "I like an arch." And you say to brick, "Look, I want one, too, but arches are expensive, and I can use a concrete lintel." And then you say: "What do you think of that, brick?" Brick says: "I like an arch."
– Louis Kahn

We can't talk about bricks without talking about Louis Kahn talking to bricks. If there's a brick anywhere to be had, then there will be the echo of "I like an arch" rattling around somewhere. Kahn, author of monumental, functionalist modernism, and who died in a bathroom in New York's Penn Station, must haunt all masonry, whispering, like a lover desperate to please, "What do you want?"

Imagine Kahn, with his black frames and floppy shock of white hair, appearing in front of the brick-clad Guild House in Philadelphia by Venturi and Rauch, an early icon of what would become Postmodernism, and being baffled by the thinness of the architects' masonry arch – a wide-mouth span topped by a symbolic antenna. Materiality and authenticity replaced by signifier. The facade is barely one brick thick, like a wrapper. Does this postmodern brick even desire an arch? Or is it more closely related to the bricks on album covers, a trope that, ever since Pink Floyd's abstracted brickwork of *The Wall*, Elton John's trompe-l'oeil *Goodbye Yellow Brick Road*, or Michael Jackson's *Off the Wall* (a back alley in Hollywood), has worn impossibly thin. [MZ]

79.
Brick wall pattern

Of course, this is years before the Ramones would make the brick wall the iconic cover for their 1976 debut album. [MO]

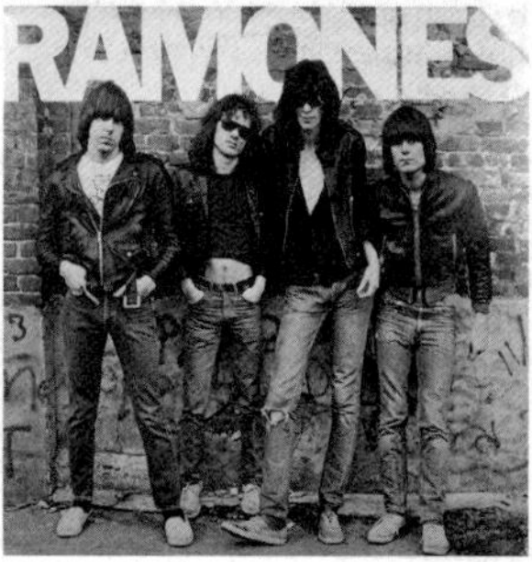

80.
Esoteric protestant sects

Let's have done with the myth of punk as white people's roots music. Let's trace it back to the blues, and forward through the other innovations of Black music that sound out the possibilities of inhabiting space as they unfold in modern times. In parallel to the punk rock being formed in the early '70s in cities like Chicago, Detroit, and New York, was the encounter of Black music with street level tech beyond the electric guitar. Let's center the story of the rise of house, techno, and hip-hop instead. Of the three, the hip-hop strand interests me the least, as it hewed a lot closer to straight masculinity. House is gay Black space-making sonics. Techno emerged out of the most deconstructed of all modern cities, the sound of fugitive basements. Both have ongoing Black avant-gardes, and have spaces within them for queer and trans bodies. The rave is still a site of experiment in 21st-century space-making. That's the story that needs to be told here. [MW]

81.
Short sharp shock

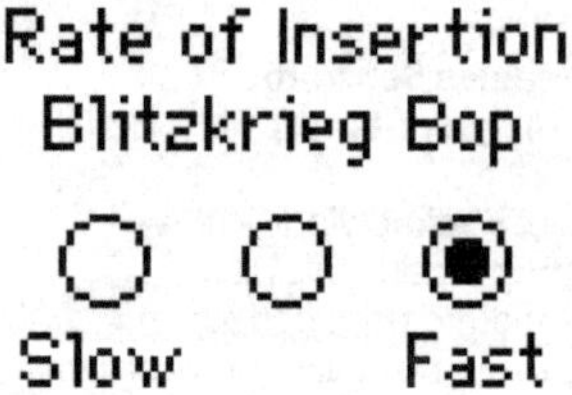

[SM]

82.
Truth in both models

Indeed, this dialectic seems to have been something that was felt at time by the participants themselves, captured perhaps most clearly in Derek Jarman's now-classic 1978 film, *Jubilee*. [MO]

83.
Modernism

"Punk" was the appropriation of gay culture, humor, and style or "camp" by the rock 'n' roll scene.

In the US, it was ignored, widely despised, and ruthlessly marginalized, but in the UK it caught fire and became a national phenomenon; its posture of provocation was well suited for Britain's subcultural tradition: sartorial youth gangs, whose participants paraded on King's Road in a cosmic style-struggle with competing fashion factions.

These subcultures were made up of teenagers who, freed from work by the "dole" (National Assistance Act of 1948), spent their time adhering to strict aesthetic tenets. Notorious English subcultures included Spivs, Teds, Skinheads, Rockers, Mods, and Punks. The English punk groups who fueled the movement were produced by that nation's art schools. The Clash, Gang of Four, Wire, the Raincoats, the Slits, Billy Childish, Monochrome Set, et al. – and more significantly the designers, scene makers, and managers who strategized the various groups' bids for infamy (Vivienne Westwood, Linder Sterling, Malcolm McLaren, Bernard Rhodes, Bill Drummond, et al.) – were indoctrinated into modernism (and modernism's stepchild, "pop art") by professors who were vociferous proponents of these two related ideological systems.

The prevalent style of the punk bands was "pop," an art movement related to modernism which simultaneously celebrated and condemned kitsch vulgarities and consumerism. It was the art manifestation of the gay "camp" ideology.

The vulgarity, shock, and black humor of punk was a short-lived sensation, though, and the next wave of groups, called "post-punk," propagated the tenets of modernism. Modernist ideas of minimalism, functionality, egalitarianism, mass production, and aesthetic leftism saw their exponent in the post-punk movement.

Post-punk is a term often confused as simply meaning after punk (like "A.D." or "middle class"), when it could more accurately be characterized as a music style with particular aesthetic and ideological characteristics. Post-punk features clean signals, without the reverb or distortion of rock, and is free of histrionics. Its lyrics are dispassionate recitations of ad copy or blasé poetry lampooning conformity, prescribed social roles, and middle-class expectations.

Post-punk groups such as Pylon revel in the mundane ("Read a Book") in their lyrics and make purposefully minimal music, such as the Fire Engines, who boasted "We never played chords and Russell didn't use cymbals or hi-hats."

A Certain Ratio, Wire, Gang of Four, and the Flying Lizards are all indicative of post-punk's art school appropriation of Bauhaus asceticism in their refutation of stadium rock's conceits of heroicism.

Post-punk's music is a "white" or European approximation of funk. It is dance-oriented and intended as "groovy" but also self-aware; spoofing protestant stiffness and rigidity. Post-punk therefore might be termed "camp modernism."

Though Modernism is thought of as a frigid rationalist infatuation with mono-class utopianism, its delinquent adherents have been legion. Mod, for example, is a shortening of "modernism." Mod disciples espoused their love for all things "continental" – or "Modernist"– in regards to design, fashion, and lifestyle. Italian scooters, espresso, and jazz music were modernist affectations common to all mods.

The mod lifestyle is like something imagined by the architects who were attempting to rehabilitate the alienation of industrial life with their egalitarian designs. Pete Meaden, early manager of the Who and mod philosopher, explained, "I was the feller who saw the potential in Mod-ism, which is the greatest form of lifestyle you can imagine – it's so totally free – totally anti-family London – in so much as that there were lonely people having a great time. Not having to be lonely, not having to be worried about relationships, being able to get into the most fantastic, interesting, beautiful situations, just out of music. You could dance by yourself, you could groove around. I saw this as a weekend."

Meaden managed the Who and re-created them as mods. In 1965, by which time he had lost control of them to another management team, the Who publicly declared their allegiance to pop art.

"We stand for pop art clothes, pop art music, and pop art behavior," said Pete Townshend (in 1965) of his band, the Who, "We don't change offstage. We live pop art."

In 1956, British pop artist Richard Hamilton defined pop art as:

Popular (designed for a mass audience)
Transient (short-term solution)
Expendable (easily forgotten)
Low-cost
Mass-produced
Young (aimed at youth)
Witty

Sexy
Gimmicky
Glamorous
Big business

The Who's avowal of pop art identity meant they had abandoned "mod" and that subculture was abandoned along with the minimal asceticism that characterized it.

Britsh subculture became more naturalistic with hippies or more florid with psychedelicism and then glam rock. Not until post-punk's emergence would modernism have a proponent in the seething mass of hormonal youth parading on King's Road. [IS]

84.
Modernism

Pete Meaden, manager of the Who, also once defined Mod-ism (and thus modernism) as "clean living under difficult circumstances."

If so, then perhaps post-modernism can be defined as "difficult living under clean circumstances." [EJ]

85.
Dozens of sub-sub-sub-cultures

The whole notion of Post-Punk has probably been our most important inspiration, throughout the years. As we already mentioned in previous interviews – it is through all the various Post-Punk subcultures in which we were involved (as kids growing up in the '80s) that we became interested in graphic design in the first place. Psychobilly, Two-Tone, New Wave, Mod, American Hardcore – it was subcultures like these that made us aware of this whole graphic sphere of band logos, record sleeves, fanzines, mini comics, mail art, mixtapes, T-shirt prints, badges, patches, etc. In a lot of our work, we are still referring to exactly this graphophere.

On top of that, a lot of Post-Punk subcultures used to have this added element of "social mobility" – which is hard to explain, but what we mean is simply this: subcultures can sometimes function as "gateways," enabling kids to escape from certain fixed social milieus. As working-class teens, growing up in non-academic surroundings, it was through subcultures such as Punk and New Wave that we first learned about movements such as Surrealism, Futurism, and Dada. In that sense, Post-Punk was a form of education for us.

And since it was through Punk and New Wave that we first learned about movements such as Surrealism, Futurism, and Dada, Post-Punk has become somewhat of a "meta-influence." It is, simply put, the influence through which we filter all other influences. Like a prism or lens, so to speak. [EJ]

86.
American Hardcore

During the spring of 1985, D.C. hardcore/punk fan and Dischord Records employee Amy Pickering sent out a series of notes in unmarked envelopes to the original Georgetown punks. These notes, assembled from cutout letters, were produced in reaction to both the increased reactionary tendencies of newer hardcore/punk bands, as well as a general disillusionment and sense of malaise after many original hardcore/punk bands had broken up. "The notes were a variation on a general theme: "Be on your toes. This is... REVOLUTION SUMMER." (quote from Mark Andersen and Mark Jenkins, *Dance of Days: Two Decades of Punk in the Nation's Capital* [New York: Akashic Books, 2003], 173.) [LL]

87.
Pluralism within Punk

Style variants minimally and intensely proliferated in early 1980s hardcore punk. In short-format record reviews in the back pages of *Maximum Rocknroll*, a super-compressed nomenclature developed to classify the deluge of new (but chronologically "post-punk") sounds. By far the most important signifier in this hardcore critical vocabulary is "thrash." And "thrash" is joined, in these short texts, to a rich array of modifiers, each of which signifies a minimal qualitative difference: hard-hitting thrash, blistering thrash, raging thrash, raw thrash, manic thrash, all-out thrash assault, stop-and-go thrash – as well as, less positively, standard thrash (which is not necessarily bad), semi-thrash, and amateurish thrash, which turns out not to be an oxymoron. There are other words for other kinds of punk sounds (garage, surf, 77-style), but being slower, this music is mostly met with the derision that the forward-looking has for any nostalgia of form. And while "post-punk" is indeed a frequently cited stylistic category in these reviews, it is a catch-all for whatever deviates from thrash, or any other easily denoted punk formula. Bands like Flipper, No Trend, or Minimal Man, who don't play fast, have cryptic lyrics, and who might write songs longer than two minutes (and might even use a saxophone or synthesizer) are sometimes okay, but are usually boring and/or pretentious.

But despite all these thrash and other hardcore variations, there is an implicit refusal of "pluralism" in hardcore punk – at least a refusal of the affirmation of pluralism as an aesthetic or ideological value. While there is an acute awareness of the micro-divisions that structure the thrash and punk scenes, and indeed in important cases (Bad Brains, Minutemen, Big Boys) there is the incorporation of "non-punk" musical elements from jazz and reggae and elsewhere, there is nonetheless the militant idea of a sharp line that divides punk from everything else. You're a punk or you're not (you're a hippie, new wave, dinosaur, metalhead, or worst of all, a poseur.) The plurality of punk is something that is only observable after the fact and apart from the movement of its actual scene. To call oneself a punk, especially a hardcore punk, is to join a collectivity and to reject all the alternatives, rather than to embrace heterogeneity and hybridity.

Punk's orientation towards singularity, in its most militant instance – hardcore – displaces the object of its agonistic politics from the "mainstream" world to the punk one; hardcore viciously circles back upon itself. While American political hardcore often took aim at Ronald Reagan, "the moral majority," the police, and the KKK, its negativity became radically self-reflexive, articulating struggles and identifying enemies within its own scenes of activity. "Nazi Punks Fuck Off" by the Dead Kennedys (1981), "Target" by Hüsker Dü (1983), "In My Eyes" by Minor Threat (1984), among many other songs (the words of which were typically printed on lyric sheets and inserted into the record in order to make the point as clear as possible) identified hardcore's political antagonists as existing within the hardcore scene itself: punks who were Nazis ("fucking Nazis!!!"), hypocrites, cynics, cigarette smokers, and/or alcohol drinkers (etc. – in a sense, the content doesn't matter.)

It should be noted that there are gentler variations in punk on this theme of self-critique: it is unclear whether "Part Time Punks" by the Television Personalities (1978) was meant to denounce or celebrate the "poseur" who becomes a punk overnight, alone, in front of the mirror. This particular loping, jangly, off-key deviation from the negative urgency of punk (which, we might pedantically note, seems to depend on the valorization of the bourgeois individual-as-shopper) was belatedly picked up in a major way in the postmodern, indie-rock, neoliberal 1990s by bands like Beat Happening and Pavement, who tried to earnestly or ironically affirm the "punkness" of the individual non-punk-conforming poseur.

But turning back to hardcore, the political logic of its internal negative orientation is lucidly expressed in a passage from "On Contradiction" by Mao Tse-tung (1937) and later reprinted in the so-called *Little Red Book*:

Opposition and struggle between ideas of different kinds constantly occur within the Party; this is a reflection within the Party of contradictions between classes and between the new and the old in society. If there were no contradictions in the Party and no ideological struggles to resolve them, the Party's life would come to an end.

Mao recognized that the bourgeoisie would constantly appear and reappear within the Communist Party, even after the revolution, and that therefore class struggle must begin to take place within the party itself. This is indeed the life of the Party according to Mao: it must ceaselessly identify new bourgeois deviations taking shape internally, find ways to make them graphically visible (in *dazibao* or "big-character posters"), and then ruthlessly eliminate them. Alain Badiou takes up this historic 20th-century tendency towards militant self-reflexivity and formal purification, in both revolutionary communism and the avant-garde, in his essay "The Passion for the Real" (2007), which is weirdly also the title of an essay by the Dutch graphic designer Jan van Toorn (2010). Badiou considers the grotesque theatrical terror of Stalin's purges at the end of the 1930s. Why was it necessary to go through the elaborate fiction of these show trials, when everyone knew they had no basis in reality? No one actually believed that Bukharin was a Japanese spy. Why not just liquidate everybody, unceremoniously? Badiou answers: "The real is never real enough not to be suspected of semblance." What he calls "the passion for the real" is the unquenchable suspicion of the semblance, of appearance, of ideology, of form itself in the condition of politics. If everything is formally mediated by ideology, then the only true (communist) response is to radically minimize and to finally purge the very relation between representation and its referent (the real). There were thus calls to purge the Communist Party from within its center, as well as to purge all the forms of art. In the final movement of this communist passion for the real, in which no criterion could exist by which one could truly identify the real with its representation, the only certainty in the end is, tragically, nothingness: utter destruction. We might call this the "negative approach" of 20th-century communism.

This comparison is not meant to romanticize the historical occurrence of hardcore, which exhibited many retrogressive tendencies and frankly gets a little boring after a while. To dialectically conclude this footnote, let's consider "Fun, Fun, Fun" (1982) by the Big Boys (who, as Tim Yohannon wrote in the seventh issue of *Maximum Rocknroll* [1983], "bash out many musical styles with ease – thrash, funk, punk, pop, ballads, you name it"):

I'm a punk and I like Sham
Cockney Rejects are the
world's greatest band

But I like Joy Division
and Public Image too
Even though that's not
what I'm supposed to do

The Big Boys – openly gay punks who unironically recorded a Kool and the Gang song ("Hollywood Swinging") – try to minimally overcome the negation of hardcore at its origins, by insisting on a basic repetition ("FUN FUN FUN") in the opening made by the negativity or nonsense of punk's form ("you don't understand what we're trying to say"). While hardcore demonstrates a tendency towards singularity, a self-reflexive purging of its form through negation, it nonetheless leaves open, here and elsewhere, a minimal space for new content ("you name it"). [OF/JF]

88.
Graffiti

Graffiti is to the city like marginalia are to a text, like the Freudian slip is to language, like the Surrealist experience is to standard reality. Naturally, Brassaï was a big fan, documenting graffiti throughout his long career as a Surrealist street photographer. The first of these depict not spray paint but the scratching of simple figures and shapes into the stone walls of Paris. When Brassaï published a montage of them in the December 1933 issue of *Minotaure*, he compared these markings to the origins of writing, ancient signs discovered in the grottos of Dordogne and the Valley of the Nile. "This is not about playing," he wrote, "it is about mastering the frenzy of the unconscious." [LW]

89.
Punk and the city

Alongside others, including cultural theorist Stuart Hall, Dick Hebdige was a researcher at the Centre for Contemporary Cultural Studies at the University of Birmingham in the 1970s. Generally recognized as the birthplace of the field of cultural studies, an outgrowth of modern sociology, the CCCS pioneered, among other things, the analysis of the ideological dimensions of fashion. Hebdige's influential 1979 book, *Subculture: The Meaning of Style*, analyzed in detail the importance of dress in the construction of marginal and resistant identities, through the study of subcultural formations such as mods, teddy boys, and punks.

The study of fashion as a system of signs has earlier proponents, including Thorstein Veblen and Roland Barthes. In his study of elites in the New World at the end of the 19th century, Veblen observed a phenomenon he described as "conspicuous consumption," which arose because, in the modern era, he argued, "the signature of one's pecuniary strength should be written in characters which he who runs may read."

Barthes's consummate text on the matter, *The Fashion System* (1967), is a high-structuralist appraisal of the grammar of fashion. Hebdige's work examines in particular the political dimension of such expression, specifically the tensions between mainstream and marginal cultural formations. But later thinkers give us a vocabulary better suited to describing this contested domain: developing a key concept from the Italian Marxist Antonio Gramsci, Beligian political theorist Chantal Mouffe and Argentine philosopher Ernesto Laclau propose an understanding of hegemony with a Lacanian inflection, that is, an ecology of power relations characterized by the impossibility of any enduring resolution. Dominant narratives are to greater or lesser degrees always in a state of flux, which is to say that they are always subject to contestation and change over time, and they must be actively reinforced and reproduced, even if such reinforcement and reproduction is often done with insidious subtlety. Such a conception of hegemony is well suited to the analysis of subcultures now more than ever, because it admits the full complexity of the polysemy of the many different cultural forms and the variety of political standpoints that tussle for purchase in variously uneasy constellations, or in outright opposition to one another.

Rhizomatic rather than arborescent models of analysis are important because the latent leftism of cultural studies itself might ascribe a nostalgic heroism to subcultures *per se*, valorizing these as noble tactics of resistance that stand in the face of a strategically articulated dominant capitalist narrative. Such binarism is dangerous because it is blind to the ways in which the relative center might be pulled farther to the right – by a carefully deployed pair of New Balance trainers, for example.

In her studies of contemporary right-wing subcultures and their fashion tropes, sociologist and educator Cynthia Miller-Idriss draws attention to signifiers of neo-Nazism and neo-fascism hidden in plain sight. Lonsdale, a British boxing and martial arts brand, unwittingly became a staple of right-wing youth in Europe. The brand's logotype is typically emblazoned large in capital letters across the centre chest of its T-shirts; when worn with an unzipped jacket, the sides of the word are obscured, so the garments read "NSDA," which is the initialism of the Nationalsozialistische Deutsche Arbeiterpartei, the German Nazi Party. Meanwhile, Fred Perry, purveyor of iconic tennis shirts, the eponymous brand co-created by the British sporting champion in the 1950s, has unhappily become the uniform of the Proud Boys, a contemporary far-right "western chauvinist" organization based in the US. Over the decades, Fred Perry polos have been worn as a subversive jibe directed at Britain's upper-class by its working youth, and as a mainstay of preppy culture everywhere, but today one particular colorway – black with a yellow laurel wreath and two yellow stripes on the collar – is the tacit livery of one of the more insidious factions of America's alt-right. And following a media statement by a senior executive of New Balance in support of one of then-President-elect Donald Trump's trade policies in 2016, a neo-Nazi blogger declared the company's footwear "the official shoes of white people." Keep an eye out, in particular, for the brand's premium made-in-US and made-in-UK models, many of which feature their respective nation's flag on the tongues.

The time-honored left–right spectrum may now be insufficient to describe the gamut of possible ideological standpoints, but the political dimension of the semiological field remains essentially unchanged since Malcolm McLaren and Vivienne Westwood shocked the British establishment with lewd graphic T-shirts and spike-studded leather jackets in London's Chelsea district in the 1970s. What are different today are the nuances of sartorial differentiation and the political ends to which subcultural style is being put: prevailing norms may be subject to counter-hegemonic disarticulation from both sides of the political spectrum and its various outgrowths. [BH/MP]

90.
Para-architectural structures

The UK's capital is understood to be one of the most surveilled cities in the world, with some 500,000 closed-circuit television cameras in central London. In cities around the globe, these cameras, coupled with increasingly sophisticated facial recognition technology, silently track, capture, and document our movements – they know your morning running route, the coffee shop you frequent after your run, and the laneways and back streets you take to get to a friend's house each Tuesday evening. They may fail, however, to recognize you when you later emerge with your friend, in brightly colored makeup, your visage altered and disrupted.

Hiding in plain sight is something that many would like to do, evading these pervasive architectures of observation. Computer Dazzle Vision – or "CV Dazzle," a term coined by artist Adam Harvey – is a way to avoid identification by surveillance technology, working against computer vision algorithms to disrupt these finite and well-defined instruments of electronic observation. Camouflage is nothing new: in 350 BCE, Aristotle observed an octopus's ability to change its color and skin texture to blend in with the sea floor when in danger. In the millennia since, these techniques have been applied by humans across a range of mediums (usually also when under threat). During the First World War, the US and UK navies painted battleships in geometric patterns to avoid enemy recognition – a type of camouflage known as "dazzle." Is CV Dazzle a camouflage for modern civic warfare?

Facial recognition technologies use biometrics to map facial shapes, distances between features, and unique contours. CV Dazzle disturbs this mapping. The techniques employed speak to types of camouflage found in nature, such as disruptive coloration, contour obliteration, and shadow elimination. Wearers paint their faces with geometric shapes, obscuring the ocular region and distorting calculations of distances between features. Special effects facial putty can be applied to the nose bridge to change its shape or obscure it, and asymmetric curtains of hair are applied as fringes. Head coverings or mouldings can obscure the elliptical shape of the skull, while contact lenses can change the hue or color density of an iris. In cities around the world, CV Dazzle groups covertly meet and apply such makeup, and then descend on the streets, incognito and *en masse*. Enthusiasts work in groups to test how effectively different makeup styles confuse their smartphones' facial recognition software. If a makeup style confuses their own devices, it will likely also confuse street-based cameras.

Makeup is commonly associated with adornment, ritual and costume, and carries somewhat problematic gender and cultural connotations, yet anthropologists have traced the use of red ochre in the African Middle Stone Age to camouflage used during warfare and hunting, and to the 60–61 CE blue woad face paint used by Queen Boudica's British Celtic Iceni tribe in battle.

During recent Black Lives Matter protests around the globe, detailed lists of instructions began to circulate to help protestors avoid facial recognition on the street and on social media (from captured images). These detailed instructions provide us with insights into how these technologies work, in protest and in everyday life: disable biometric scanning, including facial and fingerprint unlocking, as well as Wi-Fi and location services; use an encrypted platform to send messages and make calls; do not share images of yourself or others on social media; do not use a hashtag; consider using a "burner" phone rather than your primary device; consider using a Faraday bag for your phone, to block signals when not in use; and consider using makeup and head coverings. In Australia, protesters were additionally encouraged to download the Copwatch App, a platform developed to assist filming of police in conflict situations, primarily those encountered by Aboriginal people.

Today, beauty content is a prominent feature on social media channels; it is listed in the top five categories of the largest and most influential channel divisions on YouTube. Beauty influencers are big business: some earners see sponsorship deals and collaborations worth tens of millions of dollars per year. One top influencer, Huda Kattan (@hudabeauty), who has characterized the heavily homogenized contour trend, has 45 million followers and commands USD 45,000 per sponsored post. Due to this, these content creators are largely apolitical, steering away from anything that may unravel their carefully constructed webs of sponsorship. Yet, in 2020, we saw many beauty influencers and media platforms profile the use of CV Dazzle via tutorials and imagery to offer support to protestors during the BLM movement. A marked counterpoint to the contemporary makeup industry, CV Dazzle is a radical act of reclamation: of one's face, of one's identity, and of the freedom to move about a city without a trace. CV Dazzle highlights the problematic nature of contemporary technologies of surveillance, invisible architectures that are now part of the complex fabric of city streets around the globe, which we subject ourselves to every day, often unknowingly. [MP/BH]

91.
New Brutalists / New Romantics

See Mark Owens, "New Brutalists / New Romantics," in *Forms of Inquiry*, eds. Zak Kyes and Mark Owens (London: Architectural Association), 2007. [MO]

92.
Critical ambivalence

I think the sound of Ballardian "critical ambivalence" can also be traced through legendary Detroit techno producers Underground Resistance and the sonic spaces they opened up. After all, they had a lot more to be ambivalent about in the hyper-policed Robocop ruins of Detroit. This practice of a basement music to be performed in public in interstitial spaces, in the junkspace of the modern city – that's contemporary. As is their ambivalent relation to visibility in the atrocity exhibition of the giant novel in which we are all minor characters. [MW]

93.
Morbid fascination

Across his career of writing fiction and public commentary, Ballard oscillated in his attitude towards (sub)urban modernity, never settling on a fixed stance. On some occasions, he would talk about the "triumph of suburbia" as a kind of spiritual death, a dreadful and dreary sameness, a safety he paradoxically (and hyperbolically) characterized as "the biggest danger facing the human race." Anticipating Mark Fisher's trope of Boring Dystopia (a term for the prefab-drab look and culturally barren, bureaucratic spirit of Britain during the Blair era), Ballard suggested that "people's imaginations begin to dry out" in such an environment, which had neither the charms of the rural nor the exhilarations of the urban. "It's possible that you could find one word to describe the future, and that will be 'boring.' The future will be boring."

Many of Ballard's later novels are set among affluent gated communities and suburban bourgeois hinterlands, where the lifestyle of the inhabitants is comfortable but spiritually impoverished, breeding perverse counter-reactions of fanaticism and violence. But in other public pronouncements, Ballard would wax lyrical about suburbia. He described the catchment area between the western edge of London and Heathrow Airport – where he lived for decades – as "a zone of motorway intersections, dual carriageways, science parks, marinas and industrial estates" that "most people affect to loathe but which I regard as the most advanced and admirable [landscape and living environment] in the British Isles, and a paradigm of the best that the future offers us." Seemingly without irony, Ballard here salutes the very qualities of this new-built landscape critiqued by commentators like Mark Fisher and Marc Aubé (with his concept of the "nonplace," an influence on the "Boring Dystopia" idea), which is to say, the lack of local character as conventionally understood, the dearth of historic buildings and pastoral loveliness in the English tradition, the profusion of branded international chains and new-built structures using modern materials rather than traditional bricks or stone. Ballard celebrated the interzone's "transience, alienation and discontinuities... its unashamed response to the pressures of speed, disposability and the instant impulse... I have learnt to like the intricate network of perimeter roads, the car-rental offices, air freight depots and travel clinics, the light industrial and motel architecture that unvaryingly surrounds every major airport in the world."

This was the true new Britain, not some bygone fantasy

of village greens, stately homes in the Downtown Abbey vein, church fetes, the rolling meadows and leafy copses depicted in paintings by Constable, the ruined abbeys and castles evoked by Romantic poets such as Wordsworth. [SR]

94.
Avoiding the traditional rock formats

John Lydon once famously remarked that he modeled Public Image Ltd after a communication agency, rather than after a band.

Our own practice can be seen as a mirror image of that remark – as we tend to see ourselves as a graphic design studio modeled after a band.

A rock band is the perfect socioeconomic unit: just two, three, or four members, sharing one collaborative language. Small enough for each member to avoid being alienated from the end product, but large enough to have the psychological benefits of collectivity and solidarity.

So the model of the rock band is something we have always been interested in. The T-shirt print we created in 2001 (*John & Paul & Ringo & George*) can be seen as an example of that. The fact that we named our studio after an album by Sonic Youth, *Experimental Jet Set, Trash and No Star*, seems relevant as well, in that regard. Also, the first installation we ever created, at SMBA (Stedelijk Museum Bureau Amsterdam), back in 1998, was titled *Black Metal Machine* and revolved around a fictional band. So it's safe to say this theme has always played a large part in our work, from the very beginning. [EJ]

95.
Think of groups like Public Image Ltd

This notion of bands acting as fictional organizations also brings to mind the tactics of Provo. We are thinking here in particular of Rob Stolk, who (within the Provo movement, and right after its liquidation) came up with a whole range of (fantastically named) operations: Firma Provo, Groothandel in Images, Vereniging ter Bevordering van een Goed en Goedkoop Leven, Provo Likwiedaatsie Kommissie, Woningburo De Kraker, etc.

Another one of Rob's inventions was Anti-Reklame Buro Sneek (Anti-Advertising Agency Snake – a name that seems fully inspired by the ideas of Robert Jasper Grootveld), which became the moniker of a small group of former Provos who kept on printing using the Provo press right after the liquidation of the movement.

Under the name Anti-Reklame Buro Sneek, Rob printed a compact but interesting series of posters on various subjects. Sometimes these posters were drawn by himself, sometimes in collaboration with others (most notably Willem, pseudonym of comic artist Bernard Willem Holtrop). [EJ]

96.
Corporate turn

BANK? or PUNK?

Punk of America
Punk of New York Mellon
JPMorgan Chase Punk
Goldman Sachs Punk
Swiss Punk
Citi Punk

Community Punk
Commercial Punk
Central Punk
Regional Punk
Mutual Punk

BANK? or PUNK?

Hardcore Bank
Softcore Bank
Cyber Bank
Slash Bank
Garage Bank

BANK? or PUNK?

Rabopunk
De Nederlandsche Punk
ABN AMRO Punk
Triodos Punk

BANK? or PUNK?

Japan Punk
Japan Post-Punk
Punk of China
Internet Punk
DNA Data Punk
Soft Punk

BANK? or PUNK?
[SM]

97.
Corporate turn

All good adults go to heaven
All bad adults go to hell

All good adults go to heaven
However, they know there is no heaven

All bad adults go to hell
However, they know there is no hell
[SM]

98.
Corporate turn

Heaven
Hell
Future
Time

Originality
Authority
Equality

I am a superstition collector
[SM]

99.
Corporate turn

Once again! Laurie Anderson's song popping up in my brain: "Uugh... uugh..." Is she in a trance, or just a NYC smart ass? Her voice swirling slowly: "Paradise... is exactly like... where you are right now... only much much better." [DH]

Chapter 2

The Constructivist City, The Situationist City, The Provotarian City, The Post-Punk City

n the US in the 1970s. In these
nd other oppressed minority
take over the cities for long
et up their own version of the
cades of May. It is to this
ment and student power that I
ny next remarks, because they
n of minority revolt that could
del for the future.

at in spite of widespread talk
ppressed masses', it is the
o feel the oppression and not
exploited working class. While
ass may be oppressed in some
scious sense, most of the
accepted industrial-bourgeois
pe to ameliorate working con-
the traditional system through
representatives such as the
'arty and Trade Unions. This
citly acknowledged both by the
are very suspicious of the
utionaries and such student
ohn-Bendit, who speak of the
rities'.[1]

es much more sense to argue
minorities are alienated and,
, that in a specialized society,
the establishment, feels them-
time or another, part of a
ority group. Andy Warhol's
'in the future everyone will
fifteen minutes' means that
e alienated for the rest of the
hey are no longer famous or,
t, in a position to direct their
ny. The system that all
are fighting against is one
and self-determination have
ed by a conspiratorial class,
y ceased to exist. In a total
o conspirators exist anymore,
onsible for anything and the
can be blamed for mistakes
s 'the system'. It is this loss of
lf-determination which the
re fighting and which makes
of violence, the theatre of
py love-ins and all the rest of
joyable affair for everyone,
utraged' press (just one more

minority group). Alienation from power is total.[2]

The attempt to gain back power on a level where it is needed has not met with overwhelming success, but several examples can be cited. First of all there are the historical examples such as the anarchist communities in Barcelona of 1936–37, the Makhno Movement and the 'workers councils' set up right after the Russian Revolution. These various movements lasted for only a few years, before they lost power to the more usual forms of centralized governments. But while they did last, they proved that the anarchist principle of decentralized power was politically viable and socially desirable. More recently in France, the events of May 1968 have again proved this permanent possibility. Various Action Committees were formed which *directed the revolution* (if that is the right phrase) according to their own specific needs and situation. There was no centralized revolutionary party and, as long as the police were on the attack, no need for a leader or leadership.[3] There was just spontaneous organization and *ad hoc* aid coming from the people of Paris. After the 'events' had taken on a consistent pattern, street barricades of slightly used cars were constructed (68) and the Action Committees were formed. These met in continual discussion, were open to anyone, formulated general principles and took specific action suited to the situation at hand. Since the official means of communication were never taken over by the activists, they had to rely on their Action Committees to distribute information, publish the widely-read wall newspapers, and print, with the aid of architectural students in the Ecole des Beaux Arts, the posters of protest. The specific contribution of architectural students should not be overemphasized here, and yet, because of the strong Utopian tradition in architectural thinking, these students often played a greater role than those from other disciplines. In Italy, for instance, they were instrumental in starting the student protest and in Japan, Holland and America they were not far behind the first protagonists.

However, the important point is that the Action Committees came close to realizing

the ideal of part
only did they mee
one to participate
but each one was
they could make
went along (hori
organization). It i
the virtue of th
spontaneity; the
being as a result
street battles, sp
food and shelter
ceived *ideas* on h
made and its org
thing, the 'non-l
especially suspici
and the idea of
vanguard élite. M
were concerned
Russian Revoluti
power to the So
power to the (bu
rest of their scorn
Unions and Com
underwrote the
and attacked thei
its downfall.

Thus these exam
barriada invasion
May revolt etc.)
alternatives to t
They reject the i
election as too in
as 'the substitutio
another set of g
They propose to
by a participator
as often as need
economic power
smallest groups.

There are severa
both a technica
which are likely t
the future. As a
technical side the
equipment of co
permit sensitive
individual and
wished, it could
referendum on a
people to vote.

:mocracy. Not
ıd allow every-
initiate policy,
omous so that
n rules as they
r than vertical
y stressed that
:ees was their
.ey came into
action, specific
sities such as
d to precon-
:ion should be
:t up. If any-
.e revolt were
xist ideologies
ary party and
own polemics
ing how the
s soon as 'all
ırned into 'all
arty'. And the
l for the Trade
y who merely
: organization
nately causing

ific *action* (the
ıt protest, the
ted to explore
majority rule.
nt democratic
in their words
f gangsters for
y five years'.
ajority system
with elections
political and
trongly in the

velopments of
ctural nature
se positions in
ioned, on the
all the refined
. which could
between the
If a society
r even hourly
ch allowed all
on could be

(68) *Street barricade in France* May 1968: an ultimate in expendable moving architecture. The piles of cars bear an ironic resemblance to car dumps of consumer society.

(68) *St*
France
ultimat
moving
piles of
resembl
of consu

HE STREETS

Provo Hans Tuynman (far right) and friends during

and at the end of a 'white' demonstration

DEN HAAG
MODEHUIS

VAN HOUTEN

WASH
DERGROUND
CONST. CO.

Parades and Changes performed in the street, Fresno, California. The street can once again become the

FABRICS
BARON'S

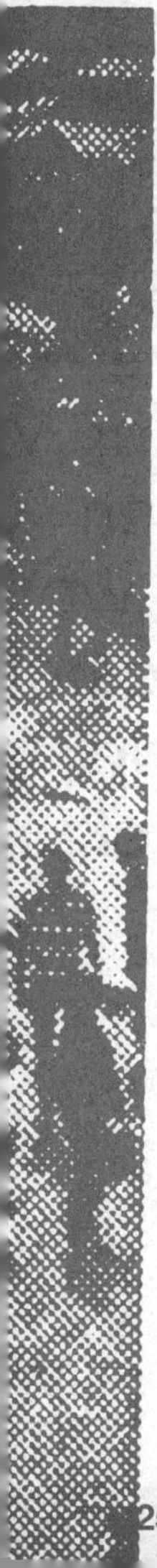

Een rol krantenpapier v
Telegraaf is van een v
wagen gewerkt en wor
gerold over het asfal
demonstratie van de s
ontaardt in vèrnielzu

De
ht-
jit-
De
ers

Alkmaar, jan. '70

WALK
TALK
WALK
TALK
WALK
TALK
WALK
TALK

May 10–11, 1968: billboard barricade.

HENRY
FONDA
SUR LA VILLE

Lissitzky, Cover for *Artists' Brigad*

ТИЧЕСКО
ЫЙ СОЦИАЛИСТ
КРАС
АР
ОПЛОТ
ВЛАСТИ
ВЕРНЫЙ
СОВЕТСКИХ ГРАНИЦ

no. 4, 1931

ФАБРИКИ ДЕР
АЙТЕ В СОЦ.СОР

Boris Ignatovich, *Nieuw Moskou,* 1931
Boris Ignatovich, New Moscow, 1931

SOLIDAIRE
de Poste

LE POUVOIR
LE

UNIS
LUTTES
FRONT UNIQUE
LES TRAVAILLEURS
VAINCRONT
LA NEGOCIATION
C'EST
LA RUSE
ADIEU...
SOLIDARITE avec les TRAVAILLEURS
ETUDIANTS
TRAVAILLEURS
LUTTENT
ENSEMBLE
HALTE
AU
TRAVAILLER
MAINTENANT
C'EST
TRAVAILLER
DANS LE DOS
nous voulons
une université
populaire
LA PRESSE
EST
TOXIQUE
CRS

TOUS UNIS CAMARADES
JUSQU'A LA VICTOIRE
POUR LA LUTTE DE TOUS LES TRAVAILLEURS
LES METALLOS TIENDRONT
TRAVAILLEURS
UNIS
FLICS A FLINS
FLICS CHEZ VOUS
.CAMARADES.
TENIR LES ATELIERS PROPRES C'EST AUSSI PARTICIPER AUX LUTTES DU PEUPLE
L'ELAN EST DONNE
LUTTE PROLONGEE
TRAVAILLEURS DE RENAULT-FLINS
LA VICTOIRE EST A NOUS
LES FRONTIERES ON S'EN FOUT!
HABITANTS
SOUTENEZ LES GREVISTES DE VOTRE QUARTIER
OUVRIERS ETUDIANTS POPULATION
LIAISON effective FLINS
L'ELAN EST DONNE
LUTTE PROLONGEE
TRAVAILLEURS FRANCAIS IMMIGRES TOUS UNIS
TRAVAILLEURS ACTIFS ET CHOMEURS TOUS UNIS

SANEREN-
SPEC

GODVERDOMME
EPORTEREN
LEREN
OP VOOR

365

COMITES D'
LA LUTTE

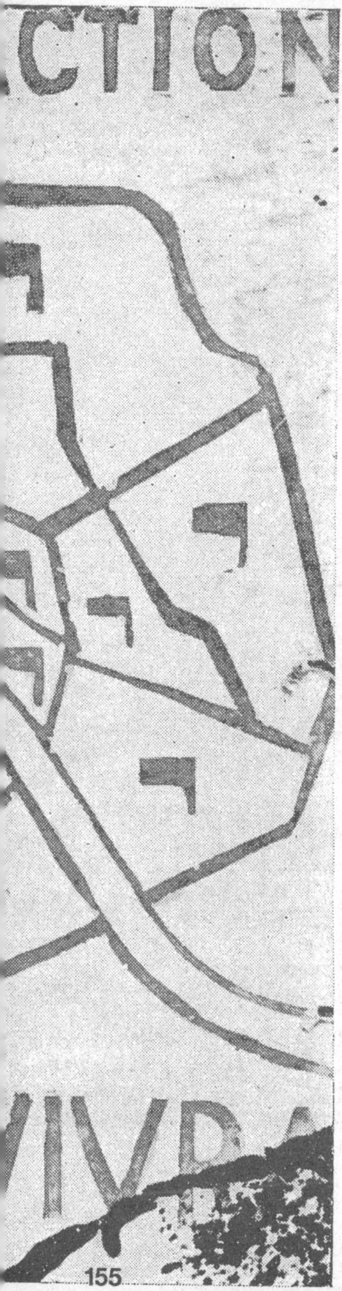
CTION

COMITE D'
TRAVAILLEU
CONTACT : C
NON A L
CAPITA

DIENST DER PUBLIEKE WERKEN SCHAAL 1:10.000

1974

KAART VAN AMSTERDAM BLAD 1

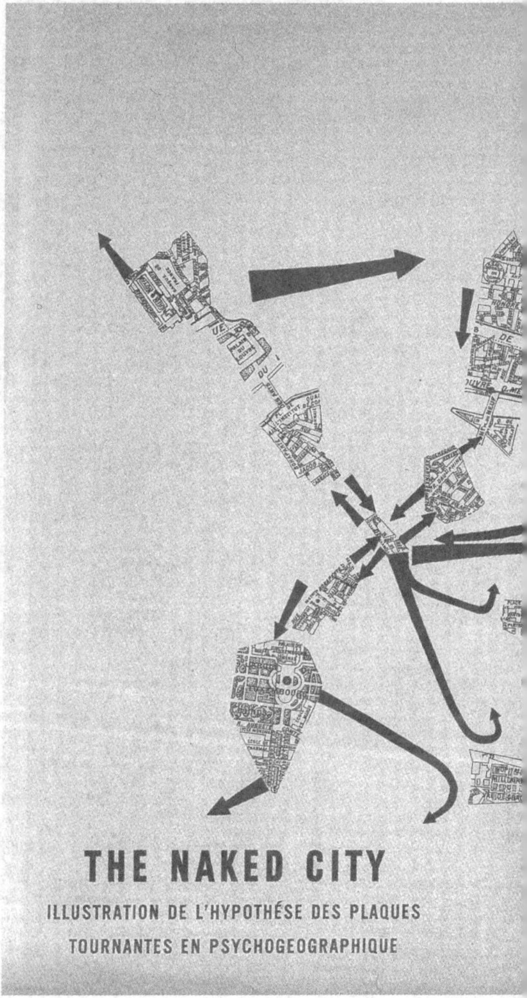
THE NAKED CITY
ILLUSTRATION DE L'HYPOTHÉSE DES PLAQUES
TOURNANTES EN PSYCHOGEOGRAPHIQUE

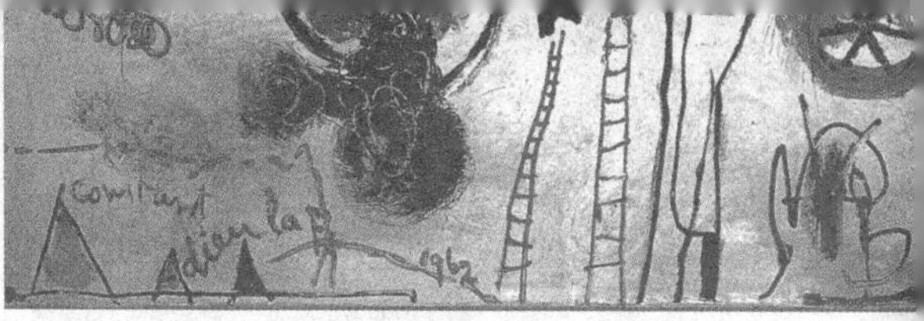

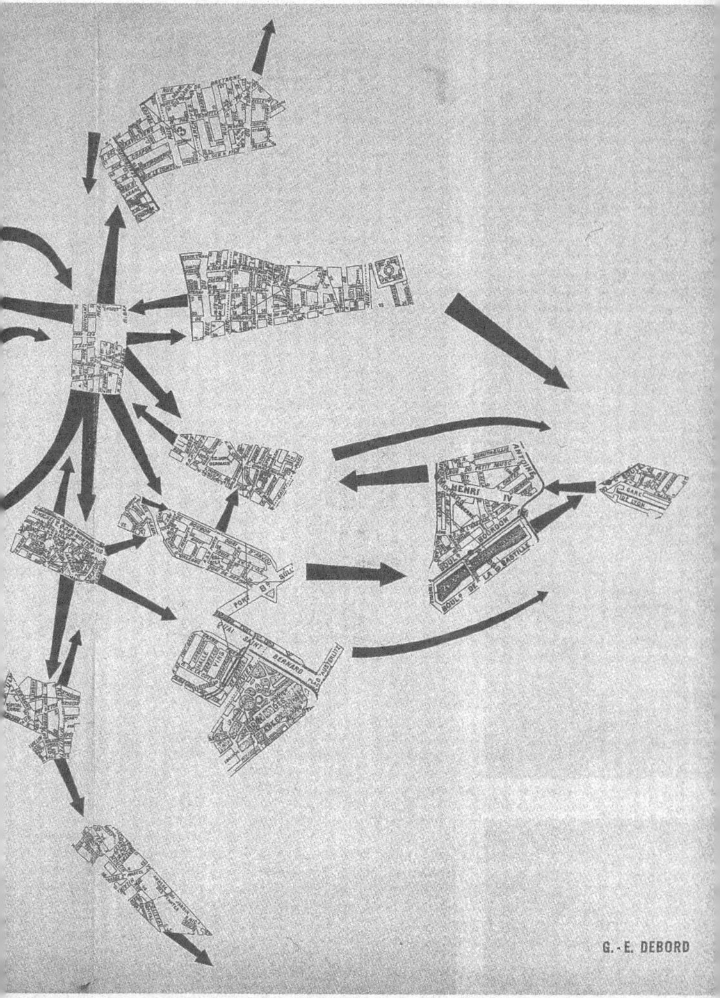

G.-E. DEBORD

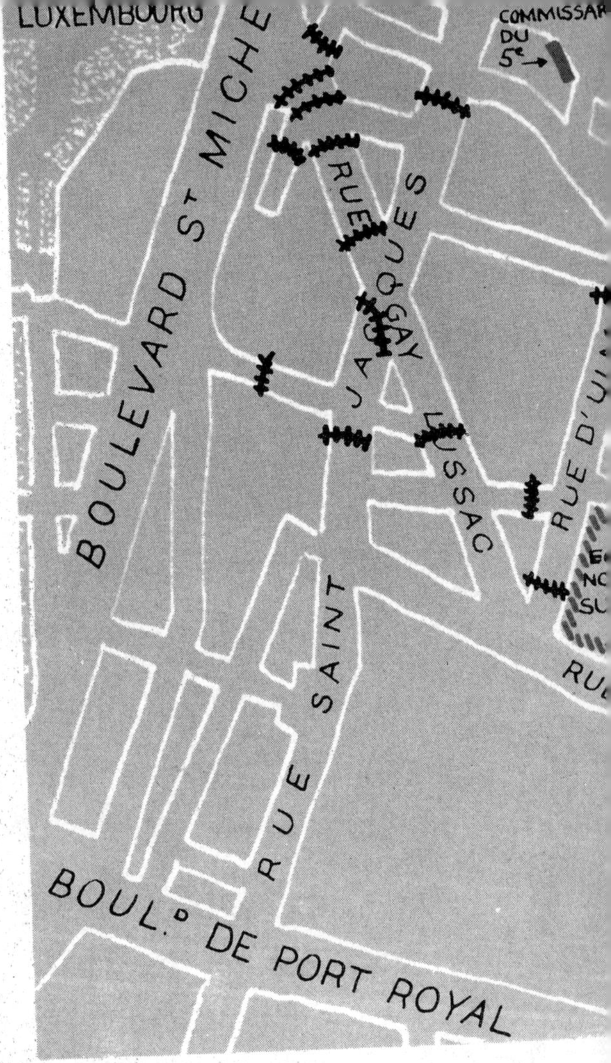

Les barricades.

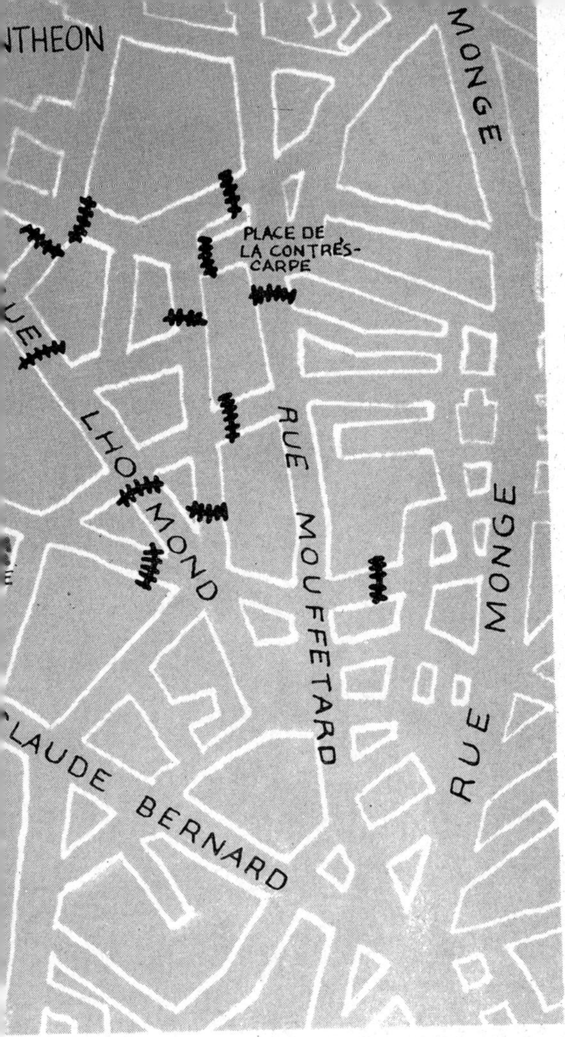

ndredi 10 mai.

over de grond gesleurd.
breekt hierbij zijn
olgens loopt een groep
getooid met bivakmutsen,
arkeergarage om die uit
Hier worden veel men-

de
en
di
gr
ge
hu
De

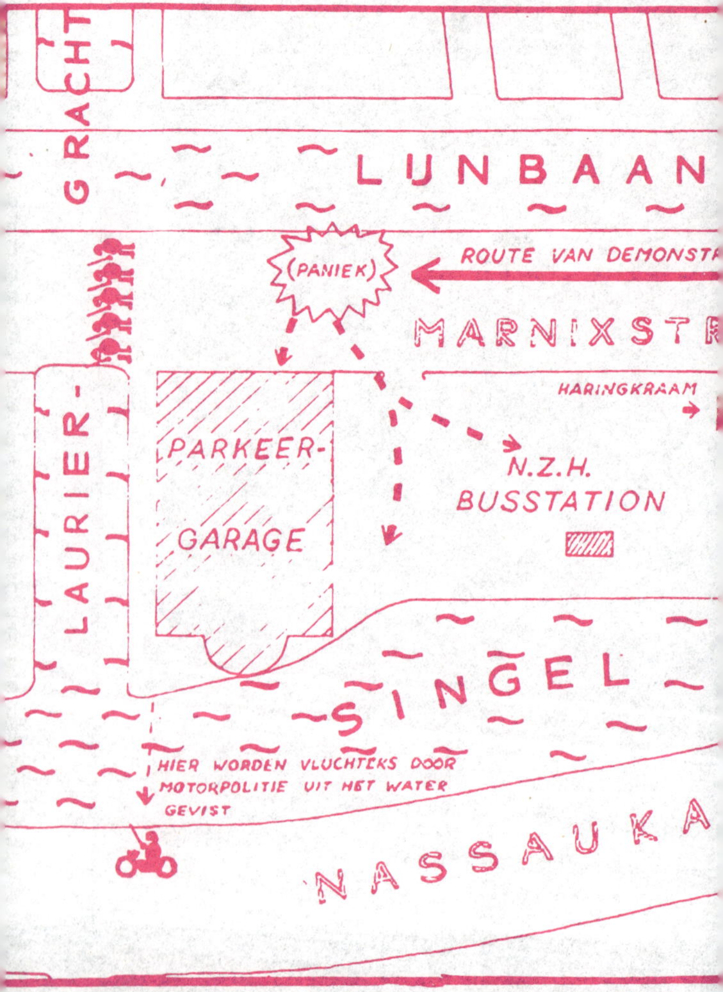

32

de hondebegeleider doet daar geen
e moeite voor. Buiten de afschei-
vorden aan de kant van de Elands-
t twee toeschouwers door een hond
en. Zij moeten naar het zieken-
vorden gebracht.
enlijke geweldpleging door de po-

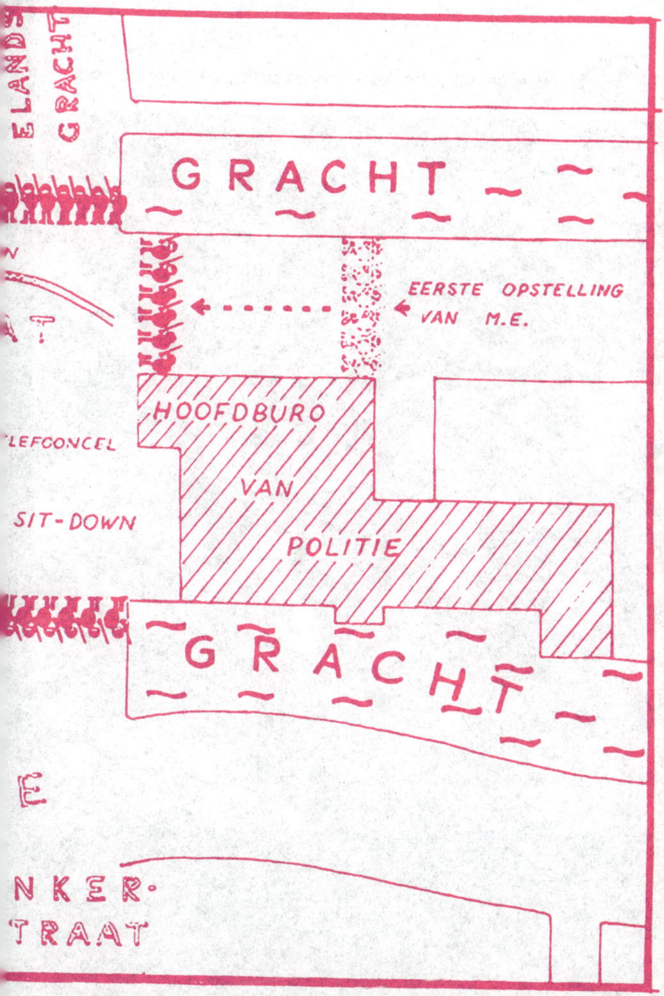

des tracts en mai 68

fondation nationale des sciences politiques / armand colin

le mur

Tatlin aveva realizzato con vari materiali libere costruzioni, per le quali più tardi coniò il termine "costruttivismo". Fin qui il suo lavoro può essere senz'altro inserito nel quadro borghese della storia dell'arte. Ma già negli anni successivi si manifesta anche in Tatlin una evoluzione frequentemente riscontrabile presso gli artisti, quando si aggregano a gruppi rivoluzionari, e la loro rivolta nei confronti dei ceti dominanti acquista evidenza. Molto presto Tatlin si mise a disposizione dei vari rivoltosi e negli anni che precedettero la Rivoluzione non soltanto patteggiò con loro, ma partecipò in maniera sempre più intensa ed esclusiva alla loro attività rivoluzionaria. Dopo la Rivoluzione, offerse sùbito illimitatamente la propria opera al nuovo governo e collaborò attivamente alla creazione delle nuove strutture educative e di una nuova prospettiva culturale. Dalla storiografia occidentale dell'arte tutte queste attività di Tatlin vengono presso che totalmente ignorate e taciute. Evidentemente contraddicono l'immagine che questa critica ha creato dell'"artista". Da noi è opinione diffusa che il grande scultore postcubista (!) si sia qui, sulla scorta delle sue convinzioni politiche, molto discostato dal proprio còmpito di artista e abbia disperso il proprio talento in problemi organizzativi. Mentre, in effetti, tale intervento sociale diretto non era per Tatlin affatto avulso dalla sua attività artistica. Anzi: era sentito da lui come una attività artistica. Questa concezione, del resto, anche dai colleghi russi non era vista senza riserve. Soprattutto Malevič non poteva essere consenziente con una integrazione così radicale nei processi sociali. Comunque, dopo la Rivoluzione, l'atteggiamento di Tatlin portò alla formulazione sostanziale delle concezioni fondamentali dell'avanguardia russa e alla aperta adesione di alcuni di questi gruppi al materialismo dialettico. La dimostrazione più evidente della posizione di Tatlin a questo riguardo è il suo progetto più ardito e più discusso: il monumento alla III Internazionale. Troviamo in Nikolaj Punin una delle prime descrizioni di questo progetto: "Nel 1919 la sezione scultura del commissariato del popolo per la cultura (Nakrompos) [a capo del quale era allora Anatol Lunačarskij; *n. d. A.*] conferì a Valdimir J. Tatlin l'incarico di progettare un monumento alla III Internazionale. La concezione di fondo di questo monumento si basa su una sintesi organica dei princípi di architettura, scultura e pittura. Si tratta di creare un nuovo tipo di costruzione monumentale, che concilii una forma puramente artistica con una funzionalità utilitaria. Sulla scorta di questo principio, l'edificio consta di tre elementi costruttivi di vetro, tenuti insieme da una complessa struttura di tralicci e spirali verticali. I singoli elementi costruttivi sono disposti l'uno sopra l'altro e hanno forme differenti, armonicamente consonanti. E potranno ruotare a velocità diverse. Per l'elemento inferiore, a forma cubica, è previsto che il periodo di rotazione intorno al proprio asse durerà un anno. Esso è riservato agli organi legislativi. Quello centrale, a forma di piramide, ruoterà intorno al proprio asse nello spazio di un mese. È destinato agli organi esecutivi (che sono: il comitato esecutivo internazionale, la segreteria dell'Internazionale e altri organi amministrativi). L'elemento superiore, infine, avrà forma cilindrica e ospiterà gli organi informativi, ruotando intorno al proprio asse nell'arco di un giorno. In esso saranno sistemati: un ufficio delle informazioni, un giornale, un ufficio per i proclami e manifesti, insomma, una centrale informativa per il proletariato internazionale. Inoltre ci sarà un ufficio telegrafico e un enorme proiettore, che proietterà su schermi di colossali dimensioni informazioni leggibili da tutti i punti cardinali. Sull'edificio svetteranno radioantenne. Le pareti esterne sono di doppio vetro, tra i due strati si crea un vuoto termostatico".

Con il progetto della torre per la III Internazionale, Tatlin pone fine alla propria attività di artista così detto "libero", cioè disimpegnato. Dopo tale progetto, egli non ha più realizzato alcuna opera d'arte in senso tradizionale. Tuttavia, si disconoscerebbe la sua posizione teorica e pratica, supponendo che dopo quella data Tatlin non abbia più operato creativamente. Il progetto in questione (che, notoria

mente, non è mai stato realizzato) è l'espressione più radicale delle sue convinzioni politiche e della sua teoria estetico-sociale. Nel suo primo manifesto postrivoluzionario (almeno, a tutt'oggi, non si ha notizia di altri), Tatlin giustifica il progetto della torre, sostenendo che esso è rispondente alle esigenze teoriche e pratiche della nuova società: "Le ricerche sul materiale, sul volume e sulla costruzione ci consentono oggi, nell'anno 1918, di combinare in forma artistica materiali differenti come il vetro e l'acciaio, i materiali di un nuovo classicismo, con lo stesso rigore del marmo nell'antichità classica. Per questa via esiste la possibilità di conciliare pure forme artistiche con finalità pratiche. Esempio: la torre della III Internazionale.
I risultati di queste ricerche sono modelli, che ci stimolano nel nostro lavoro di costruzione di un nuovo mondo e si appellano a tutti i produttori, perché controllino le forme che ci circondano nella nostra nuova vita quotidiana".
In questo primo manifesto postrivoluzionario, che si riferisce al progetto per il monumento alla III Internazionale, Tatlin pone chiaramente l'arte al servizio della società. Egli ripudia l'attività artistica disimpegnata e postula una sintesi di tutte le funzioni tecniche dell'uomo. In Tatlin, tecnica e arte non sono più disgiunte, né la tecnica è mero strumento al servizio dell'artista. Al contrario: l'immaginazione dell'artista, la sua facoltà creativa, va posta al servizio del progresso tecnico. L'artista deve rispondere con le sue particolari doti alle esigenze tecniche della nuova società. Questo utilitarismo specifico tatliniano è ancora oggi oggetto di discussione per artisti e teorici. Si potrebbe dimostrare che questa subordinazione di Tatlin a esigenze socialmente rilevanti non finisce necessariamente alla linea di montaggio di una fabbrica automobilistica. Laddove, invece, essa rappresenta la conseguenza della posizione ideologica di un artista

Vladimir Tatlin
Versione semplificata della Torre costruita sopra un carro per una grande dimostrazione a Leningrado.

Tatlin e i suoi collaboratori mentre lavorano alla costruzione del modello del « Monumento per la Terza Internazionale », 1919/1920.

Il mor
bozzet
preved
in alte
pirami
una sp
ambien

ANARCH
173
Seven-Up
FLIPTOPPEN
ZIT BARSTENSVOL
BELONING

nge mensen in de grote stad zich hebben genesteld, is ee
; ze maar tijdelijk. Ook in dit opzicht leeft de erfenis
oort.
ielden hun happenings, in politietaal 'vertoningen', met
, krenten en een witte walvis. Zij 'belemmerden' het verk
hts om 12 uur ernstig was. Zij deelden pamfletten uit op
gens de politieverordening verboden was. Zij trokken
ionument aan de Apollolaan – ze waren niet bang v
leling – dat als symbool van militarisme met witte v
rd.
as alles voor de provo's. Zij kwamen dan ook wijd en z
ad iets met macht te maken, wat zij 'image' noemden, m
met geld, want zij lieten zich door de persvertegenwo
tjesvolk contant betalen.
e een verwarrende logica. Traditionele randfiguren, bo
irrealisten, dronken clochards, vechtersbazen of inbrek
taande scheidslijn tussen hun randgebied en de gevesti
at de politie hen niet begreep, dat de burgermaatscha
at hoorde erbij. De provo's echter treiterden de gezag

ced in the Netherlands.

ant. v.d. Steen"
MET DE PIL MEER
DE PIL
EER....

ONZE

DAG ALLES STIK ZACHT
Wij WORDEN STINKEND RijK

Heinz Mack, Otto Piene, and Günther Uecker, carnival processio

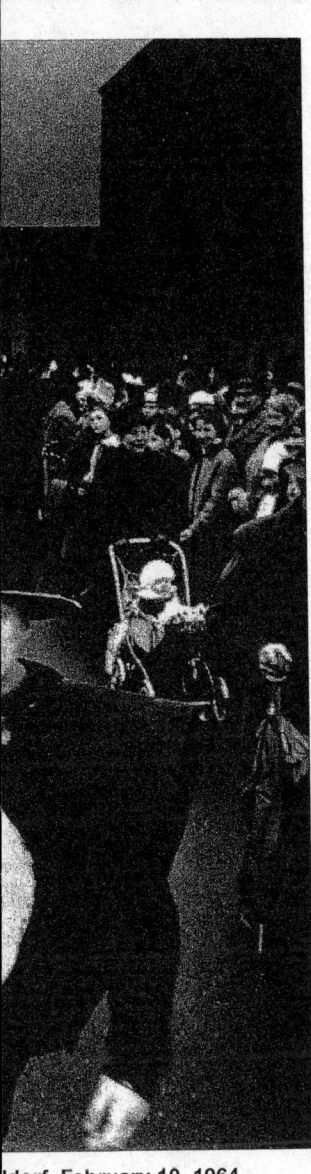

ldorf, February 10, 1964

Cosey Fanni Tutti and Genesis P-Orridge in *Towc*

 movements had received subst

e Crystal Bowl, Galleria Vittorio Emmanuele, Milan, 1976.

l funding

Richard Cork

PROVOOS IN NEW BABYLON
ambiance de jeu
gemeentemuseum - den haag

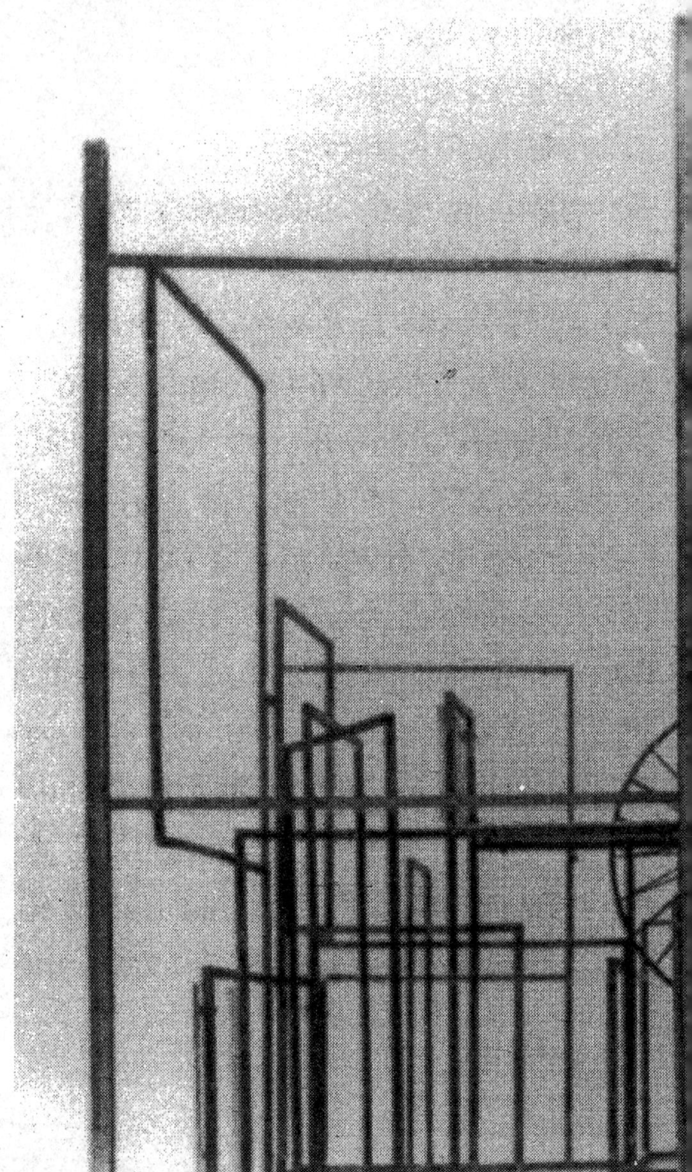

PANDJE
194

BEZET EEN PANDJE
ONTRUIM JE EIGEN HUIS
ZET ONZE KINDEREN NIET IN DE KOU!
DEPANDENCE HOTEL DE GERSTEKORREL
ZO ALS DE WAARD IS VERTRAPT HIJ ZIJN GASTEN
BROOD- EN BANKETBAKKERIJ
van Til
WARME BAKKER
DEURWAARDER

maandag 25 februari
buro IJtunnel

PARADISE NOW

ever Work"

our own space and time, can
uty can only be a beauty of *sit*
al, and *lived* . . .
he Situationist International w

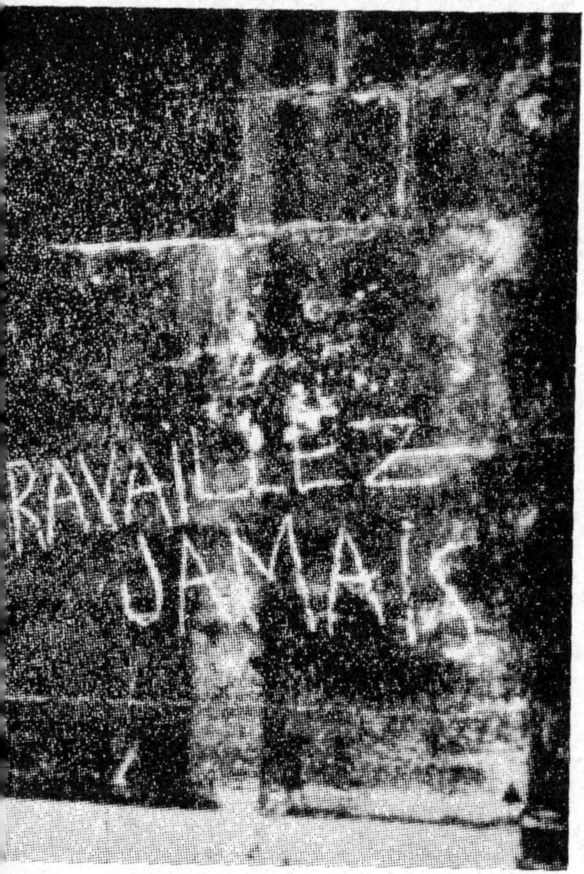

"Pr
uat
scri
de
the
jac
mo
virt
dati
calli
aga
not
The
abo
mos
une
Ger
to t
that
I.S.

ke it happen. The new
n, which is to say provi-

ounded on the conviction

IMAGE

at

uit-
con-
sse-
be-
in
ngs-

ad-
rre
am-
aar
ol-
die
dijk
een
de

de
ter-
resi-
gaal
kie-
be-
de
len.'
pre-
en
ost-

dom
SSE

)

7

van

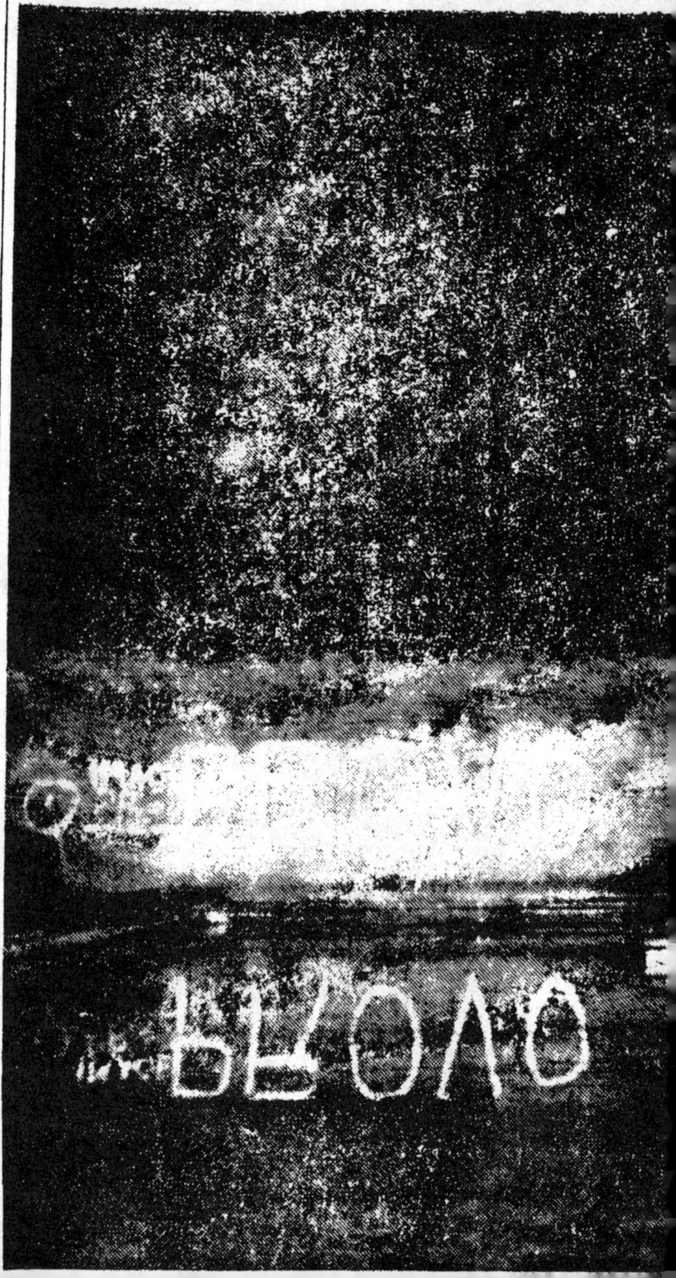

besmeurd

PRO

1012

iep in
ebouw
or de
d door
figuur,
de tot
binnen-
kleur

ieuwe
veren
over-
oude?
itken-
voor
nieuw

nieu-
m el-
duide-
kaars
steeds
en.

, 5, 6,
26, 27,
37, 38,
52, 54,

41, 42
22, 23,

Kazim

alevich *Suprematistische wolkenkrabber*, 192

WY WILLEN EEN
MET BUURTEN
WONEN, SPELEN,
LEREN EN
VLAKBY EN
GEBEURT VOOR
OUDE MENSEN.

NIEUWMARKTBUURT
WONING VERLIES
DOOR OORLOG 366
10 JAAR SANERING 353
NOG VOOR METRO 115
NIEUWBOUW '46-'74
6 WONINGEN

Een gedeelte van een kleurproject in de Amsterdamse Nieuwmarktbu

CRITIQUE DE L'URBANISME (Supermarket à Los Angeles, août 1965).

rique s'est aussitôt penchée sur cette nouvelle plaie. Depuis plusieurs mois, sociologues, ns, psychologues, économistes, experts en tous genres en ont sondé la profondeur... pas un « quartier » au sens propre du terme, mais une plaine désespérément étendue tone... « l'Amérique à un étage », toute en largeur ; ce qu'un paysage américain peut avoir morne avec ses maisons à toit plat, ses boutiques qui vendent toutes la même chose, ses s de « hamburgers », ses stations-service, le tout dégradé par la pauvreté et la crasse... ation automobile y est moins dense qu'ailleurs, mais celle des piétons l'est à peine plus, habitations semblent dispersées et les distances décourageantes... Le passage des Blancs us les regards, des regards dans lesquels on lit sinon la haine, du moins le sarcasme (« En- enquêteurs et autres sociologues qui viennent chercher des explications au lieu de rnir du travail », s'entend-on dire souvent...) Quant au logement, il peut sans doute élioré matériellement, mais on ne voit guère comment il sera possible d'empêcher les e fuir en masse un quartier dès que des Noirs commencent à s'y installer. Ces derniers ront de se sentir laissés à eux-mêmes, surtout dans cette cité démesurée qu'est Los dépourvue de centre, sans même la foule où se fondre, où les Blancs n'entrevoient leurs es qu'à travers le pare-brise de leurs voitures... Le pasteur Martin Luther King parlant quelques jours plus tard et appelant ses frères de couleur à « se donner la main », quel- ia dans la foule : « Pour brûler... » C'est un spectacle réconfortant de voir à quelque dis- Watts des quartiers dits de « classe moyenne » où des Noirs de la nouvelle bourgeoisie leur gazon devant des résidences de grand confort. »

Michel Tatu (**Le Monde,** 3-11-65).

qui, aussitôt, dément la ratio- oppresive de la marchandise, t apparaître ses relations et rication même comme arbi- et non-nécessaires. Le pilla- quartier de Watts manifestait isation la plus sommaire du e bâtard « A chacun selon x besoins », les besoins dé-

ment rejette. Mais du fait que cette abondance est prise au mot, *rejointe dans l'immédiat,* et non plus indéfiniment poursuivie dans la course du travail aliéné et de l'augmentation des besoins sociaux différés, les vrais désirs s'expriment déjà dans la fête, dans l'affirmation ludique, dans le *potlatch* de destruc-

ver
an
ier

966

de
nd,
ven

tici
ge-
en
ge-
Mel-
het
we-
ja-
aar
ond
er-

nk-
ma
de
tot
de
end
aire
hte
ati-

en
eld-
dse-
heft
een

966

Bakou – 1922 "Concert pour sirènes d'usines et sifflements de fum

dans la galerie Barbazanges : la musique devait faire part
l'ameublement permanent de la salle, à la manière du m
lier. Trois brefs morceaux sont joués parallèlement pa
musiciens au nombre de 23. Aujourd'hui nous pou

Le chef d'orchestre se tient sur le toit d'un grand immeuble

Le pianiste David Tudor créa l'œuvre : il était assis au piano et bougea trois fois les bras pour indiquer que le morceau avait trois mouvements. Cage déclara que les bruits que l'on pouvait entendre pendant ce temps étaient sa musique.

Bier

GEVEKE WARMTETECH

cla

14 Kasimir Malewitsch, Suprematistisches Architekton, um 1926

Monument am Anfang,
ıus am Potsdamer Platz, 1921

15 Georges Vantongerloo, Interrelation von Volumen, 1919

56

35 *Tyrannical Tower* 1961, unique bronze, 72 × 22 $\frac{3}{4}$ × 15 in. Collection Mrs Gabrielle Keiller, Surrey

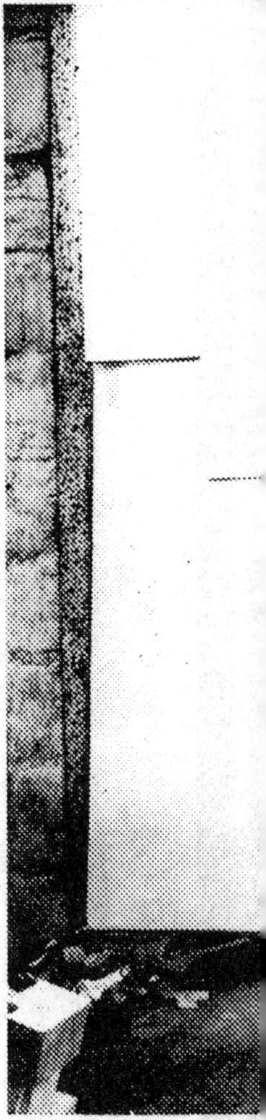

36 *Town Tower* 1[illegible]
77$\frac{1}{2}$ × 17 × 22 in

32 Erich Mendelsohn, Hochhausskizzen, 1922

und Autos, andererseits aber auch als allg
prinzip, das er mit seiner Architektur w

Mendelsohns Entwürfe weisen besonder
spektivische Untersichten, skizzenhafte A
Details, Verzicht auf städtebauliche Kon
Baukörper, die meist abgerundete Kant
bei den Arbeiten der Mitglieder der „Gl

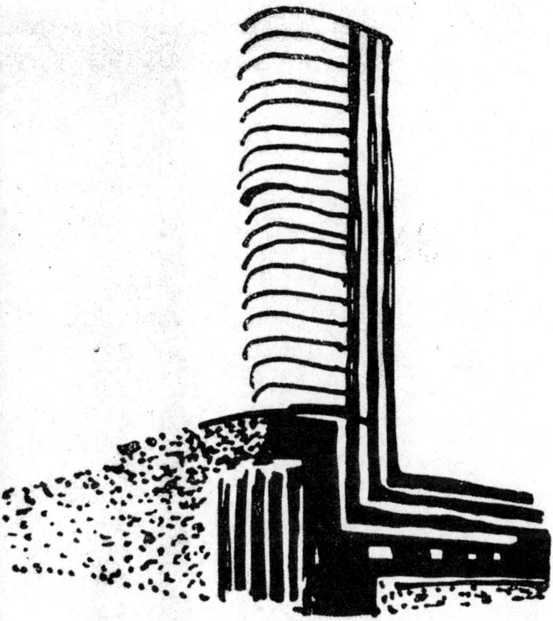

›3 Hans Scharoun, Skizze eines nicht eingereichten
Entwurfs für den Bahnhof Friedrichstraße, 1922

„Vitalität“, ein universales Lebens-
:geln wollte.[157]

cteristische Merkmale auf wie per-
n, klare Kontraste, Vermeidung von
›wie plastische Durchformung der
veisen. Kristalline Elemente – wie
Kette“ – fehlen völlig, ebenso or-

s McLaren, 'because that's what his friends had. He ıe first girl he met: he was sacrificial and I think it's resents it, but he's accepted it. It was the same with first girl, got her pregnant and ended up by living en years. I settled down as well, but I wouldn't allow grow around me completely. I did at least in my own reate an environment I could run wild in. I did try.'

3

In the autumn his account o centre for mil community w Mods'. In thos are now. 'It w anywhere else

His first teac Theodore Ran enjoyed meeti their achiev

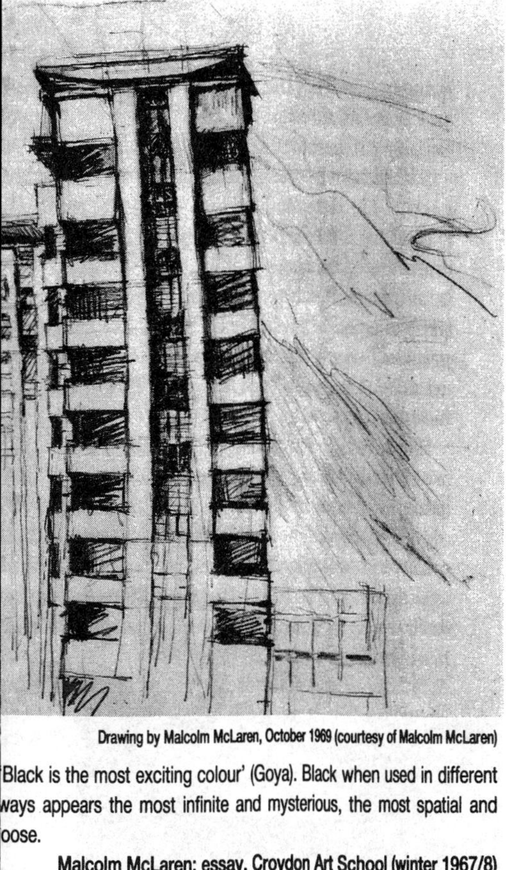

Drawing by Malcolm McLaren, October 1969 (courtesy of Malcolm McLaren)

'Black is the most exciting colour' (Goya). Black when used in different
ways appears the most infinite and mysterious, the most spatial and
oose.

Malcolm McLaren: essay, Croydon Art School (winter 1967/8)

, Malcolm went to Harrow Art School, which, in
en's early life, Fred Vermorel describes as 'the
nd for Bohemian frenzy, mixing the local gay
tniks, drug pedlars, sexual delinquents and
art schools were less result-orientated than they
place where everybody went who didn't fit in
Malcolm; 'it was a brilliant hangout.'

s a dapper, aristocratic Royal Academician called
idn't enjoy teaching very much,' he says, 'but I
curious suburban generation. In a lot of cases,
s to liberate themselves from their background.

200

Enrico Prampolini, Futuristisch paviljoen op de Internationale Tentoonstelling, Turijn 1928.

Fortunato Depero: *"Padiglione del libro"* in the
"III Mostro Internazionale delle Arti Decorative" (Monza, 1927)

7

Today, if we wish to realize the compositional Utopia latent in this tradition and seriously disregard all material fetishist games, the individual linguistic constituents of language and writing must trade in the tradition of these literary conceptions. On the other hand, we must attempt to compose reading processes and progressions which were unknown to the literature of the past. To put a fine point on it, reading itself must be recomposed; perception itself consequently autonomized and reoriented.

Visually perceptible literature must not dissolve into letter-graphics or remain shiny letter-painting on the way to itself. It is not a potpourri of typographical methods which exist for their own sake. It is not merely a tolerable literature, *en passant*. Its

exandra Exter, Vera Mukhina en B. Gladkov, *Paviljoen van het tijdschrift*
estiva Tsik op de landbouwtentoonstelling in Moskou, 1923

D
o
jo
vo
co
St
1
vo
ci
In
op
vo
br
on
op
be
ui
ho
bl
de
od
Ko
pi
ui
en
id
"s
Zo
de
th
av
he
no
kw
ve
de
He

ПРОЛЕТАРИИ

…А С [illegible]АТЕРИАЛАМИ [illegible]
…РЕТЬЯ ФАКТИЧЕСКИЙ ФАКУЛЬТЕТ ГДЕ СРЕДСТВО…
…ОИТЕЛЯ ЯВИТСЯ ТЕХНИКА. ЗАДАЧА [illegible] ШКОЛЫ…
…ТИ УЧЕНИКА НА ПУТЬ ТВОРЧЕСТВА И ИЗОБРЕТЕ…
…ДЕЙСТВИЮ СОЗДАЮЩЕМУ НОВЫЙ УТИЛИТАРНО-
…ЧЕСКИЙ МИР, ЭЛЕМЕНТЫ КОТОРАГО ПРЕДН…
…А СУПРЕМАТИЗМ.

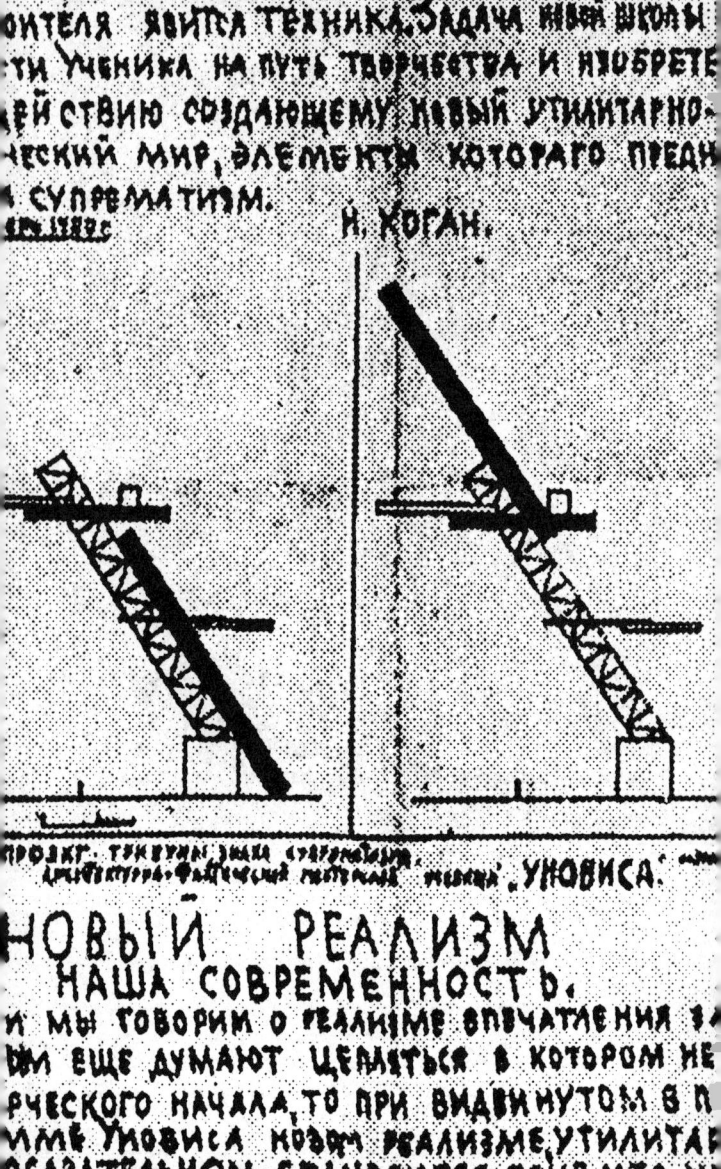

[illegible] Н. КОГАН.

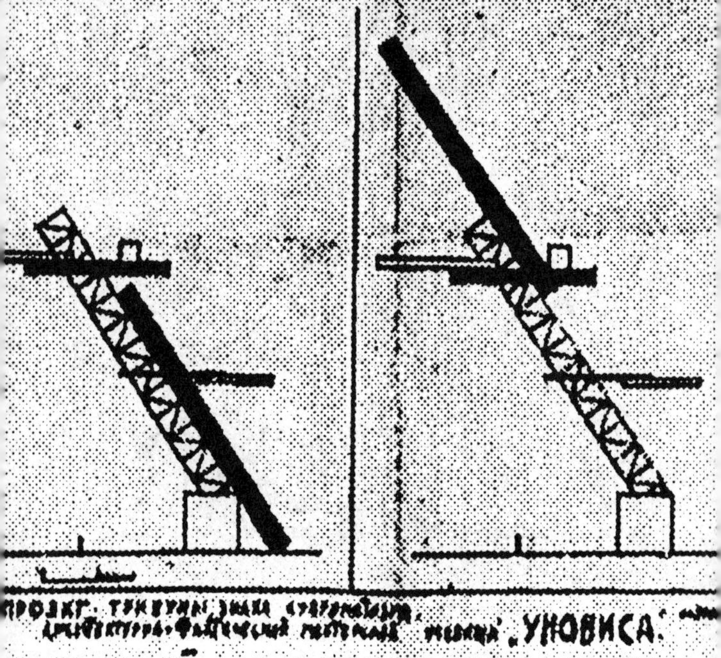

ПРОЭКТ ТРИБУНЫ [illegible] [illegible] АРХИТЕКТУРНО-ФАКТИЧЕСКИЙ [illegible] [illegible] „УНОВИСА."

НОВЫЙ РЕАЛИЗМ
НАША СОВРЕМЕННОСТЬ.

…И МЫ ГОВОРИМ О РЕАЛИЗМЕ ВПЕЧАТЛЕНИЯ [illegible]
…[illegible] ЕЩЕ ДУМАЮТ ЦЕПЛЯТЬСЯ В КОТОРОМ НЕ…
…РЧЕСКОГО НАЧАЛА, ТО ПРИ ВИДВИНУТОМ В П…
…ИМЕ УНОВИСА НОВОМ РЕАЛИЗМЕ УТИЛИТАР…
…ОСАЗАТЕЛЬНОМ, СТАНОВИТСЯ ЯСНО, ЧТО Н…

[illegible]

литературном,
живописном,
архитектурном,
или строительно-техничес-
ском.
…ны быть даны
…рукописей.
…рных случаях с мотивировкой
…мя, возраст и адрес должны быть указаны
…е анкеты.

1921

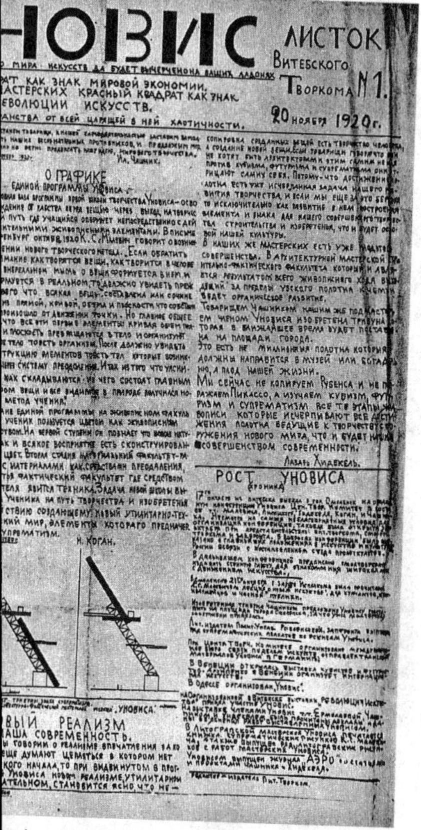
…НОВИС

Листок Витебского Творкома № 1.

20 ноября 1920 г.

…о мира искусств да будет вычерчено на ваших ладонях.
…рат как знак мировой экономии.
…астерских красный квадрат как знак.
…еволюции искусств.
…анства от всей царящей в ней хаотичности.

Ил. Чашник.

О ГРАФИКЕ

…единой программы Уновиса…

Товарищем Чашником нашим же подмастерьем членом Уновиса изобретена трибуна, которая в ближайшее время будет поставлена на площади города.

Это есть не миллионные полотна которые должны направится в музей или богадельню, а плод нашей жизни.

Мы сейчас не копируем Рубенса и не подражаем Пикассо, а изучаем кубизм, футуризм и супрематизм все те этапы живописи которые исчерпывают все достижения полотна ведущие к творчеству сооружения нового мира, что и будет нашим совершенством современности.

Лазарь Хидекель.

РОСТ УНОВИСА
(хроника)

Н. Коган.

…вый реализм
…наша современность.

…ember 1920, Vitebsk

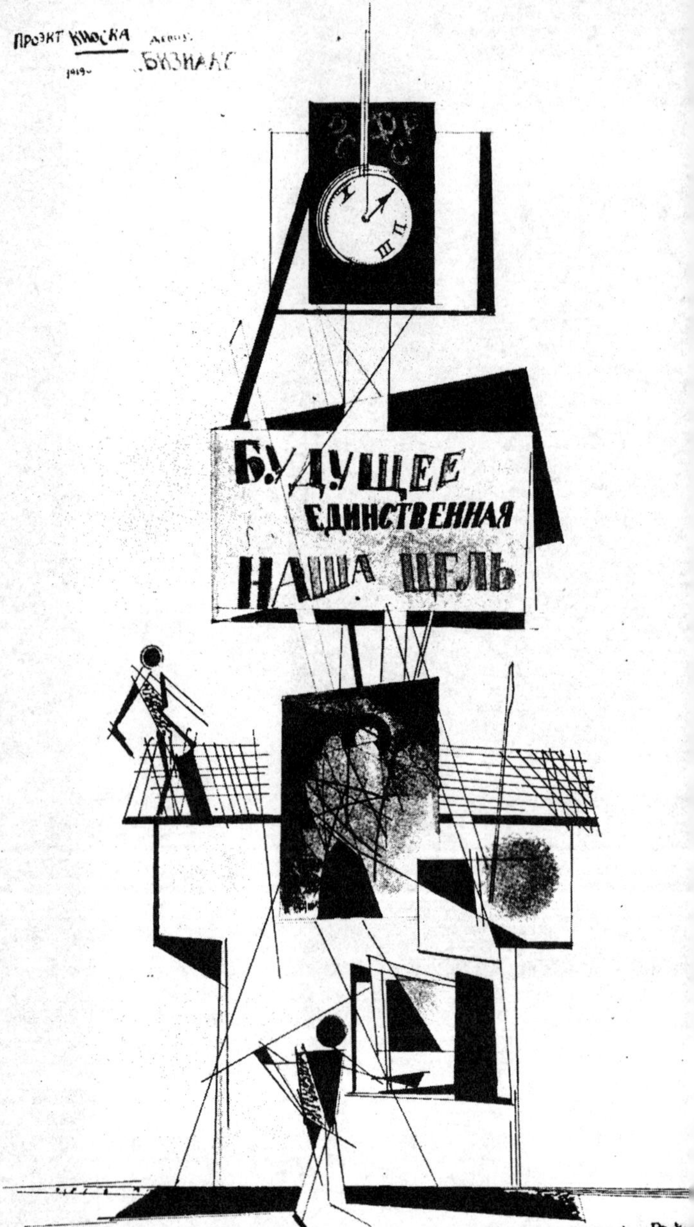
ПРОЭКТ КИОСКА
1919
БУДУЩЕЕ ЕДИНСТВЕННАЯ НАША ЦЕЛЬ

dspeaker no. 3. 1922
l ink on paper, 7 1/16 x 5 5/16"
)
ch of Comrade Zinoviev
the artist's wife, V. I. Kulagina

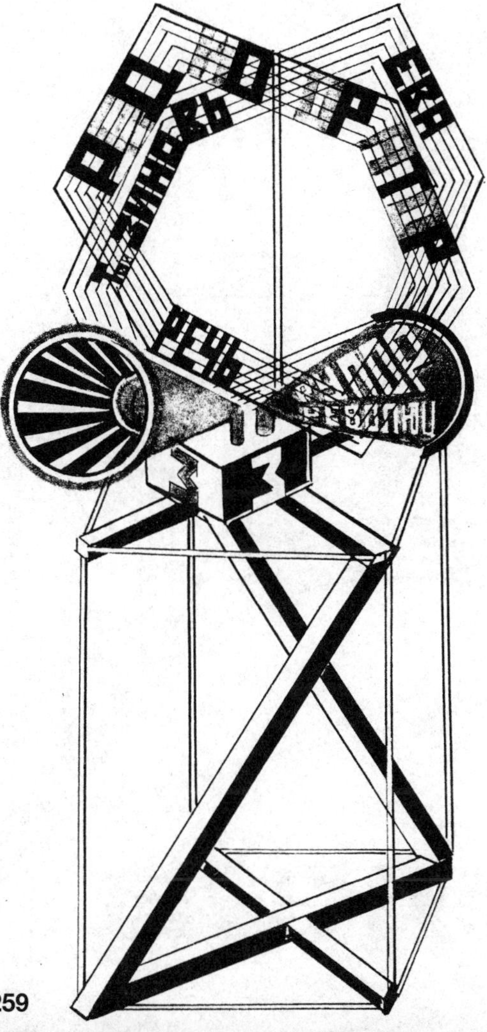

WKGB

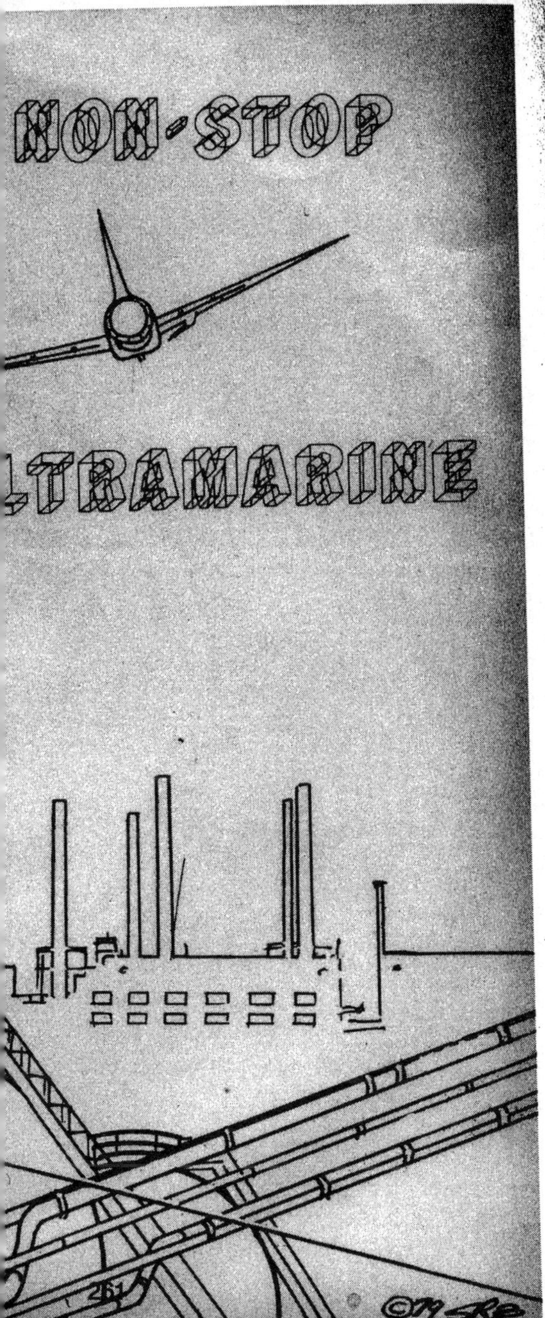
NON-STOP
LTRAMARINE

, 1885–1953)
ik III
ent to the
onstruction,

akis

1885–1953)
Pamiatnik III
ent to the
:0

264

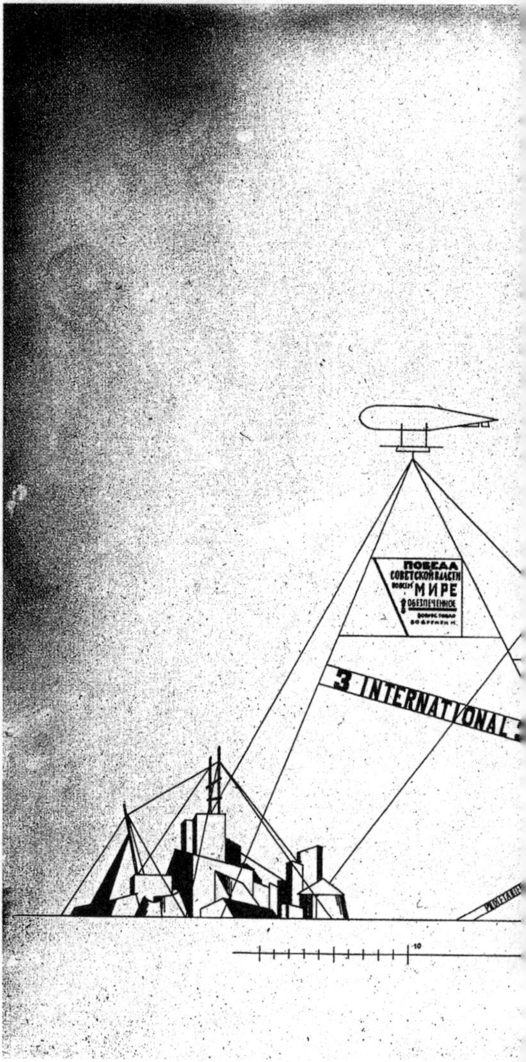

265

3
VIVE CI III
ПРОЛЕТАРИИ ВСЕХ СТРАН
III КОММУНИСТИЧЕСКИЙ ИНТЕРНАЦИОНАЛ
ОСВОБОЖДЕНИЕ РАБОЧИХ
ДЕЛО САМИХ РАБОЧИХ
PROLETAIRES de Tous Les Pays
III КОМИНТЕРН III
КОМТРУД
30
40
50
60 c.

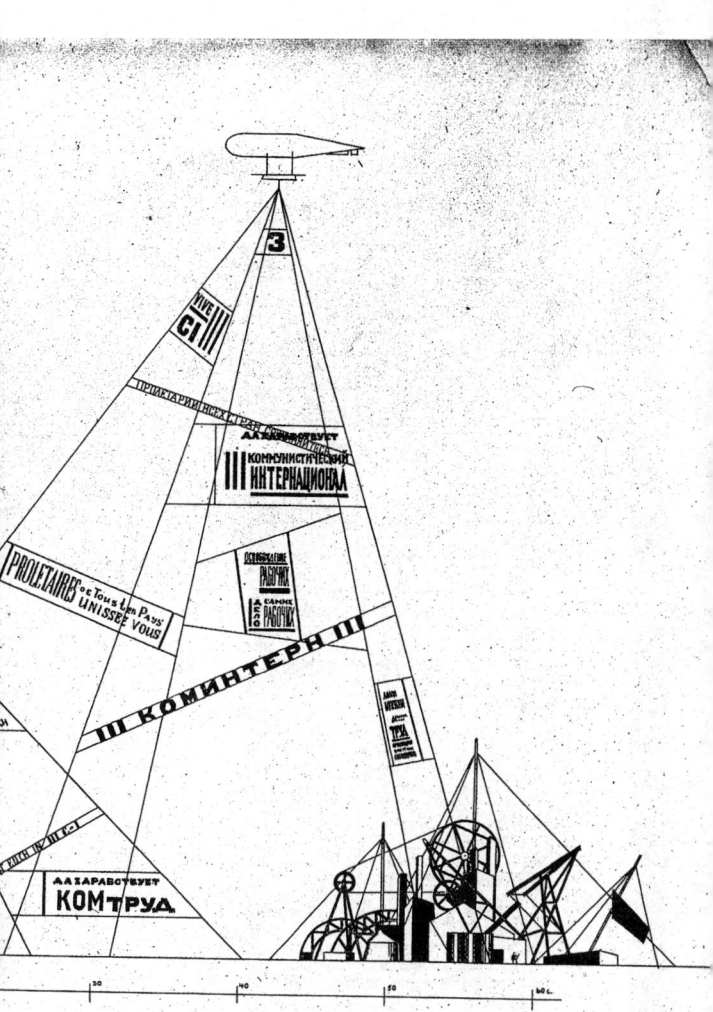

ects based on an open system begin as a neutral field into which a variety of clip-on,

tem), desig manufactu

96

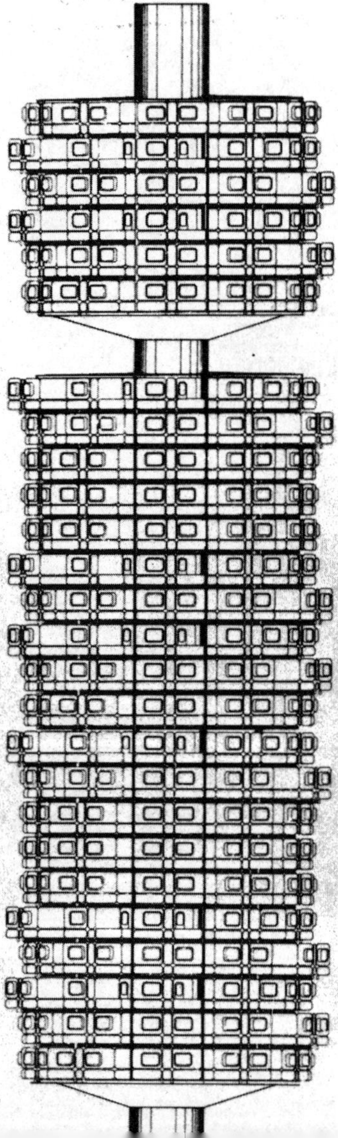

97

Kisho Kurokawa and
e Taisei Construction

tem is that it affords greater variety in floor-plan layout than the traditional sh[e]
wall system.

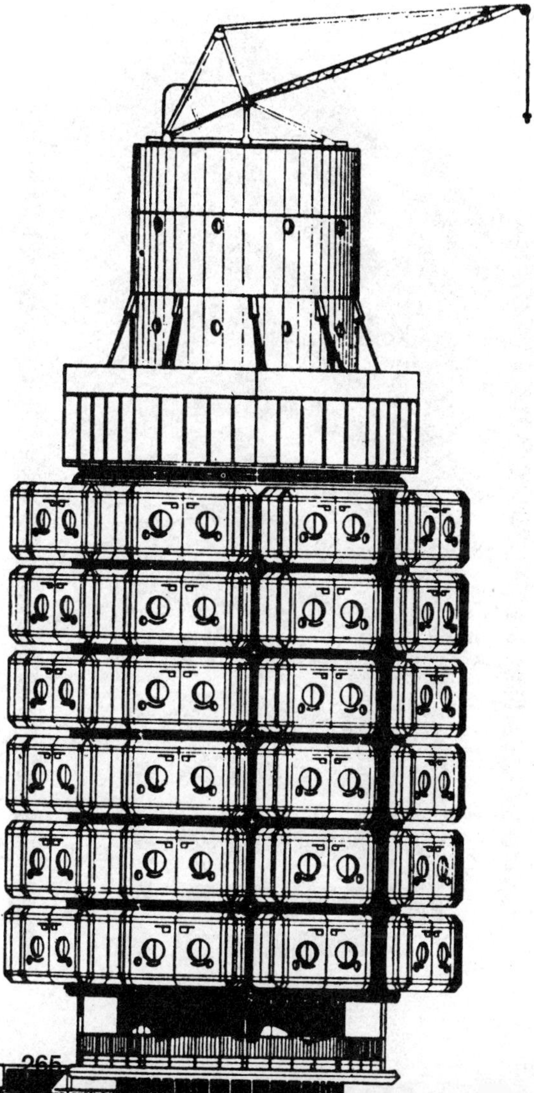

c

d

389

CHELSEA
HIGH RISE LIVING

DUB HOUSING

SCREAM W
45RPM

TH A VIEW

Here Comes the Future

EN

CITY FUN

10 P

S THE MODERN WORLD

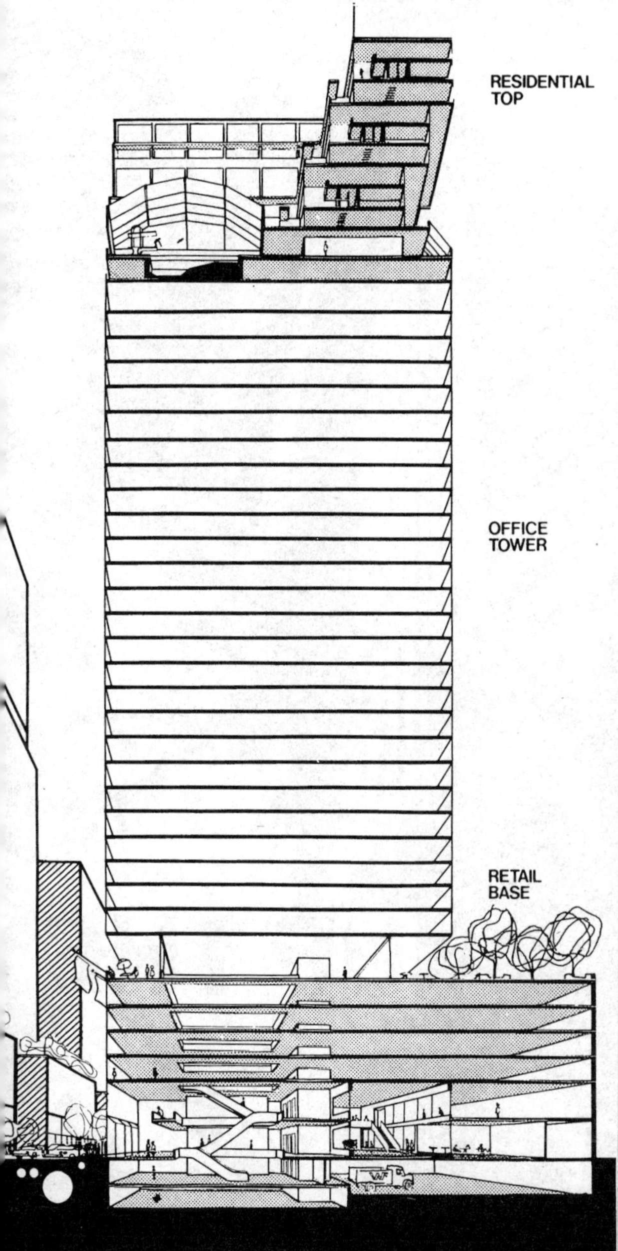

▲ Typerende indeling van wolkenkrabber op

De vo
instelli
gen va
scherm
van de
York er
bevord
grote v
tailhan
band h
bijzond
unieke
leggen
markan
omring
ren var
de pub
met inb
Te bevo
op de r
bruikt,
grond
gehoud
opbren
gesteld
Onder
de Fifth
zelfde
die de s
Zoals ir
trict he
showrc
maatsc
gronda
gens de
gen de
wordt e
vloerop
het geb

UP THEY

RISE
Sex

4) И дом

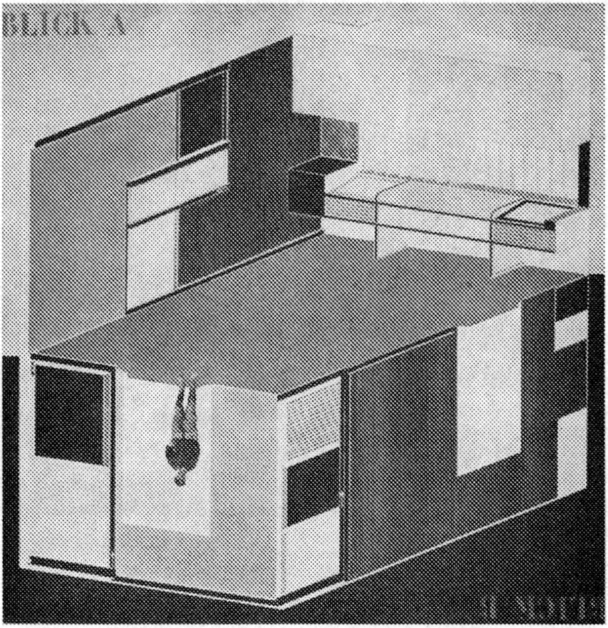
BLICK A

241

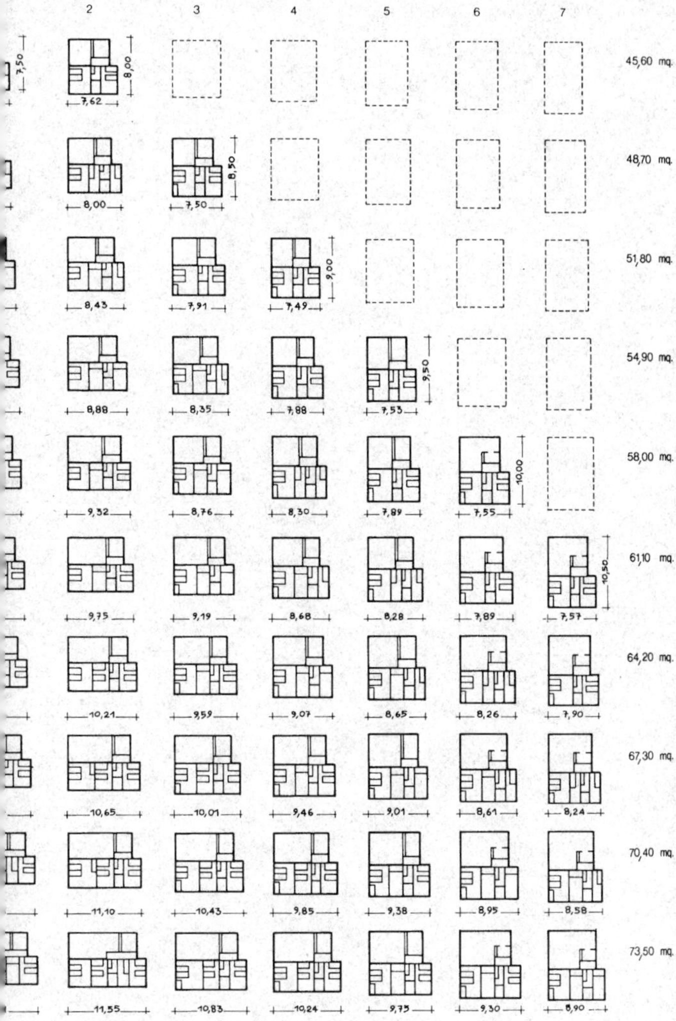

. Klein, *Typologie van de bestaansminimum-woning*, 1929.

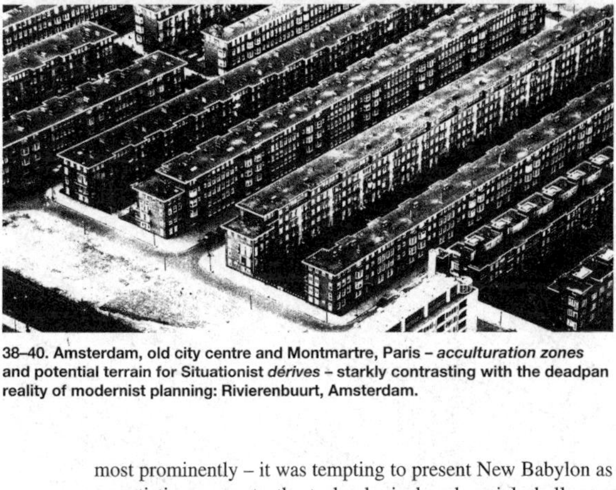

38–40. Amsterdam, old city centre and Montmartre, Paris – *acculturation zones* and potential terrain for Situationist *dérives* – starkly contrasting with the deadpan reality of modernist planning: Rivierenbuurt, Amsterdam.

most prominently – it was tempting to present New Babylon as an artistic answer to the technological and social challenges posed at the end of the 1950s (another of these would be the population explosion). Indeed Constant, for obvious reasons,

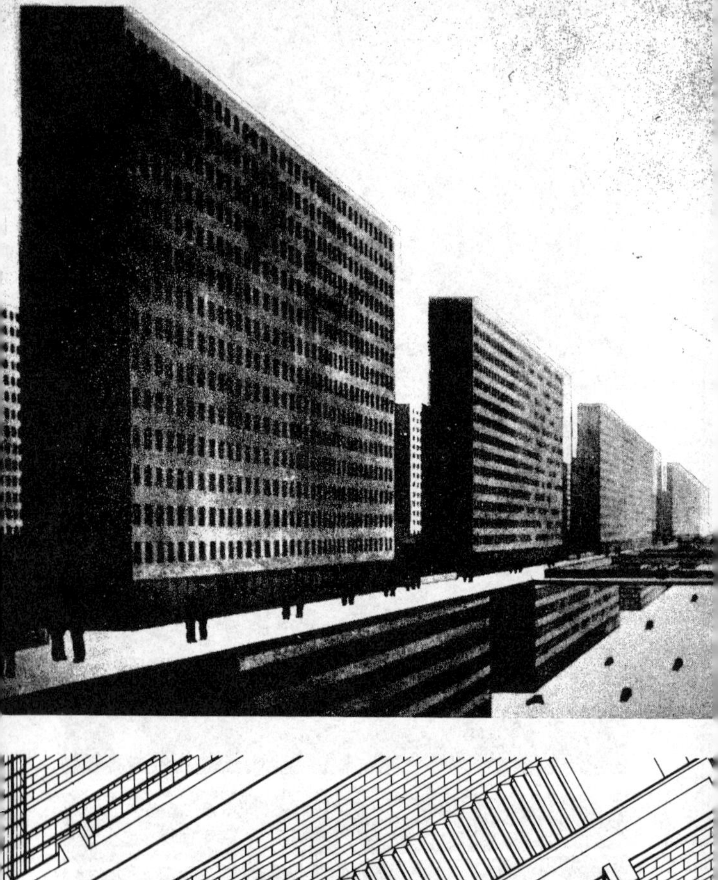

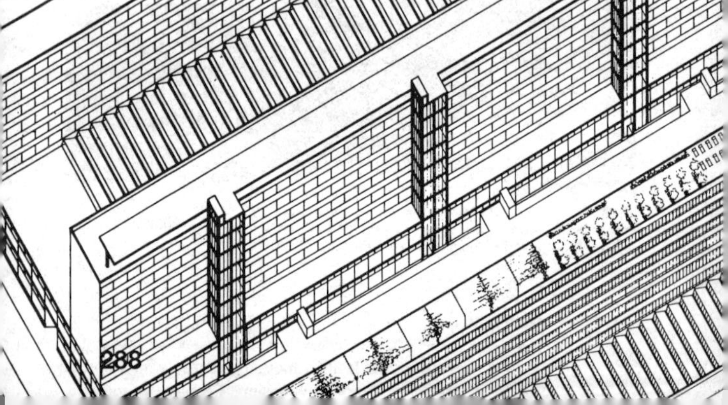

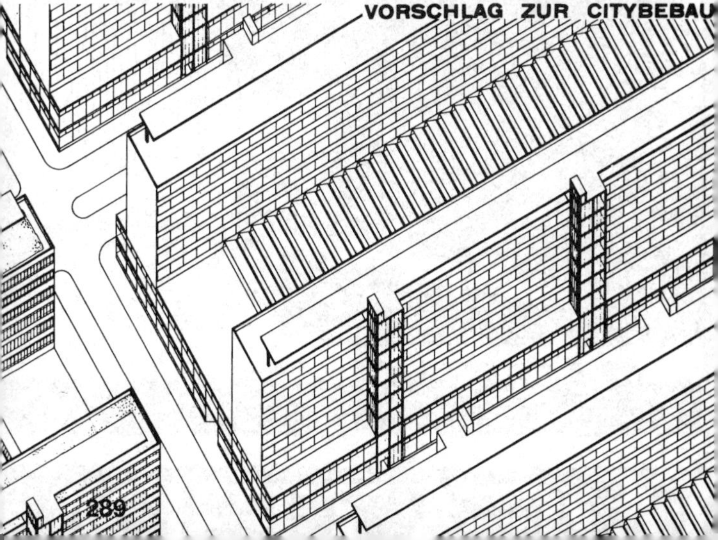
VORSCHLAG ZUR CITYBEBAU

DAM
ON THE

AGE
OKTOBER

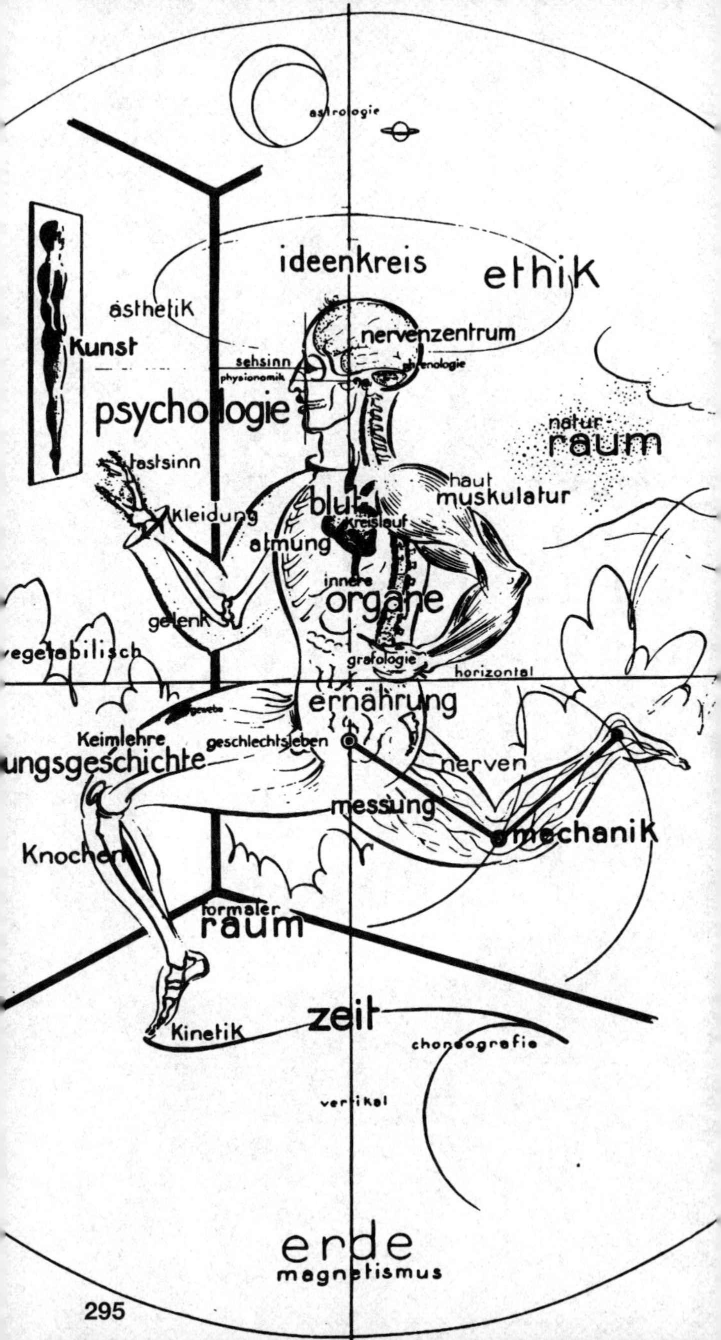

astrologie
ideenkreis
ethik
ästhetik
nervenzentrum
Kunst
sehsinn
physionomik
psychologie
natur-
raum
tastsinn
haut
muskulatur
blut
kreislauf
Kleidung
atmung
innere
organe
gelenk
vegetabilisch
grafologie
horizontal
ernährung
Keimlehre
geschlechtsleben
ungsgeschichte
nerven
messung
mechanik
Knochen
formaler
raum
zeit
Kinetik
vertikal
erde
magnetismus

BRAVE NEW WORLD
NEGATIVE DIALECTICS
ADORNO

ONE
DIMENSIONAL
MAN
MARCUSE

CITROËN CLICHY
1000F MINI
ROËN NANTERRE
ATION GENERALE
SALAIRES
NOS 40H
RETRAIT
NTER

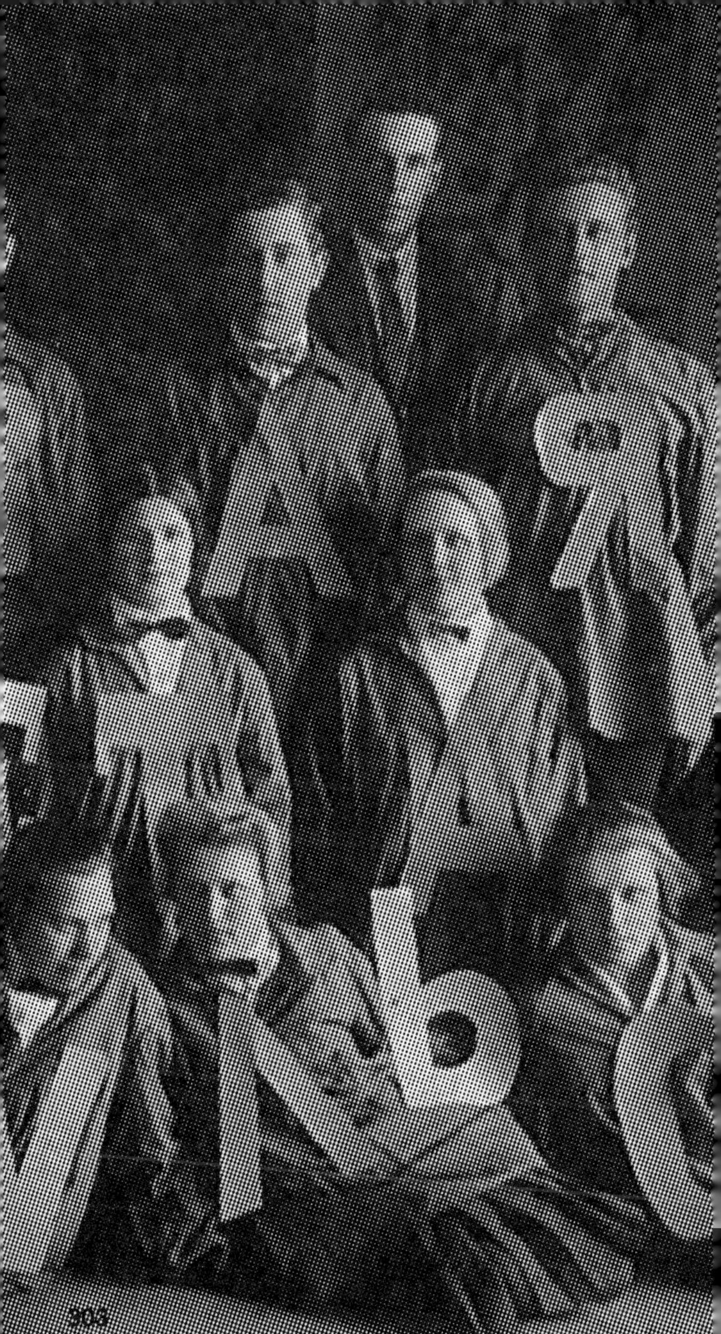

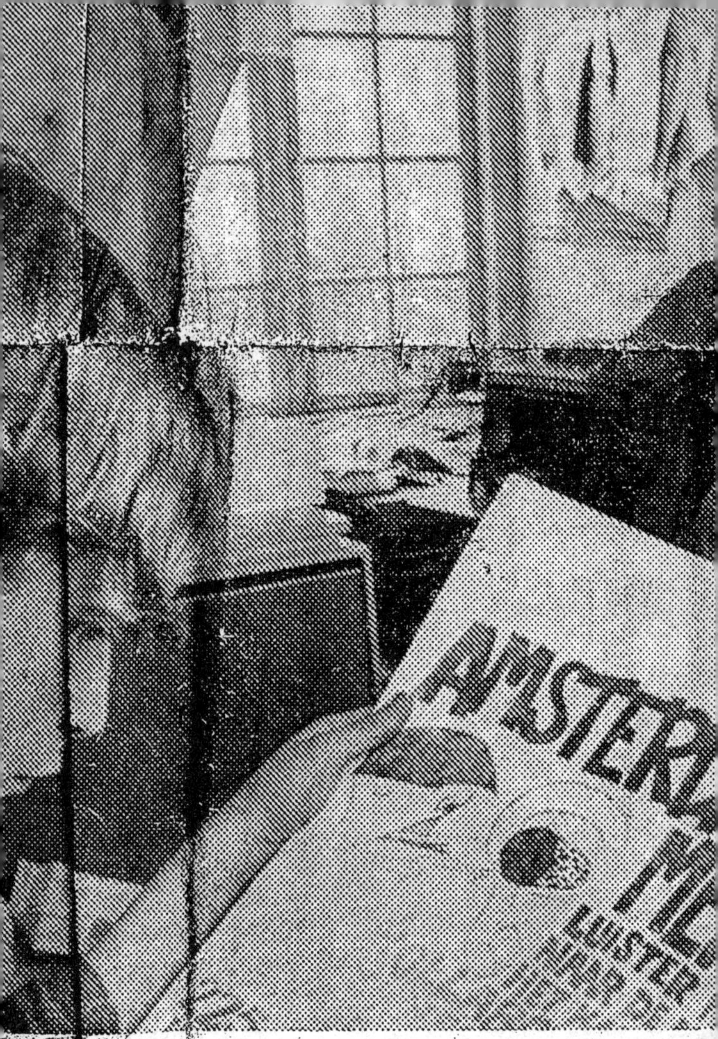

is klaar
de strijd

(ADVERTENTIE)

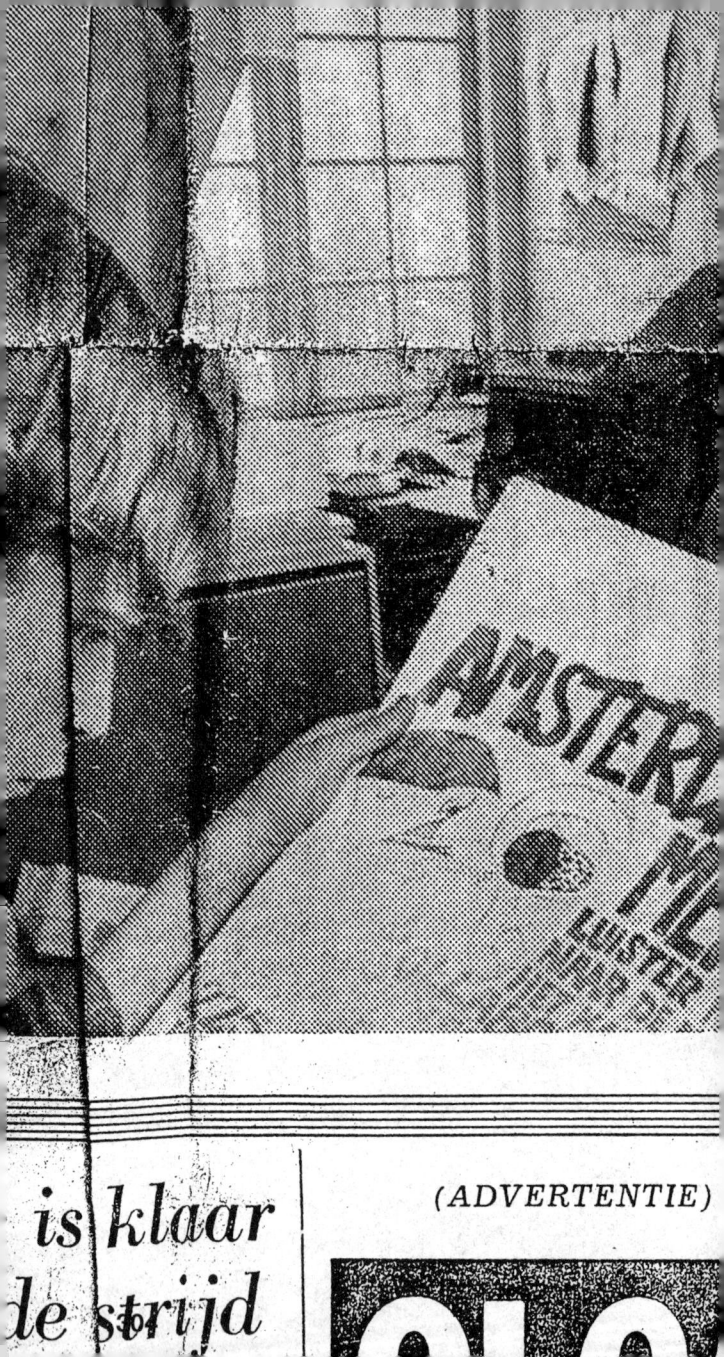

SPOEDIG GES

Van ee

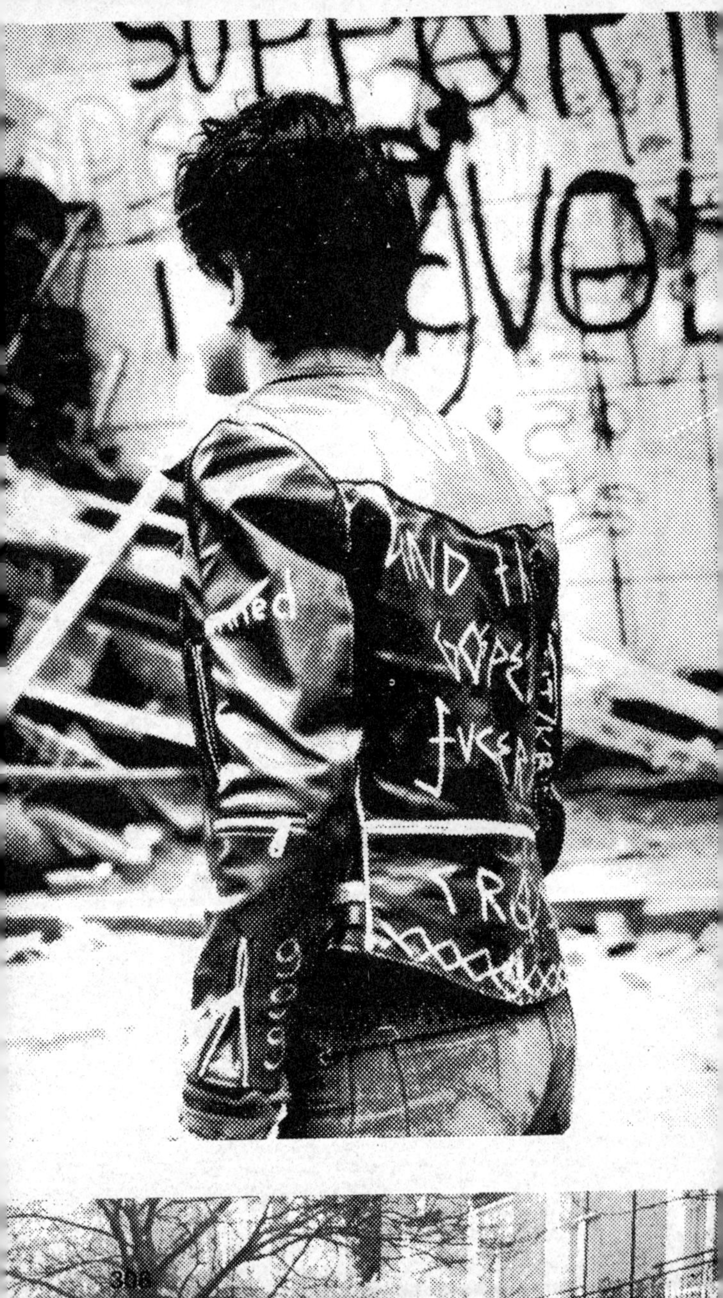

FROH

MERDE,
bourgeois

PROVO

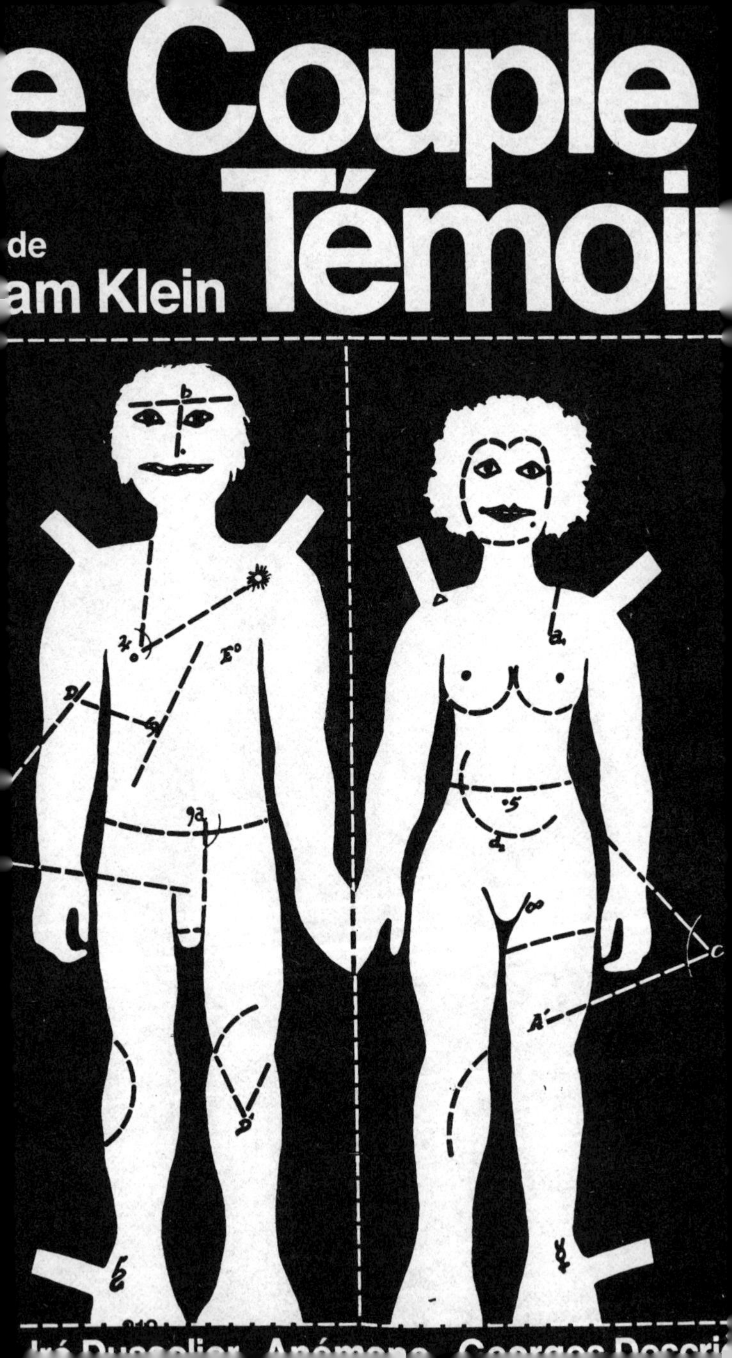
e Couple
Témoi
de
am Klein

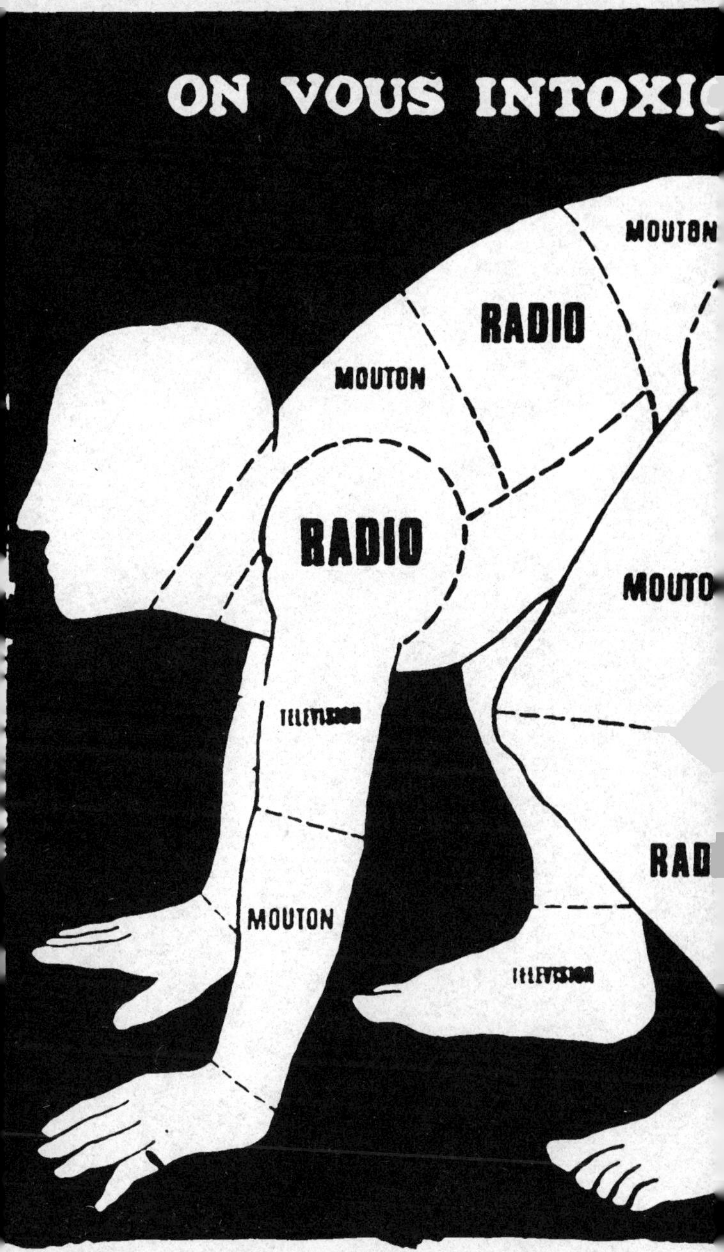
ON VOUS INTOXI
MOUTON
RADIO
MOUTON
RADIO
MOUTO
TELEVISION
RAD
MOUTON
TELEVISION

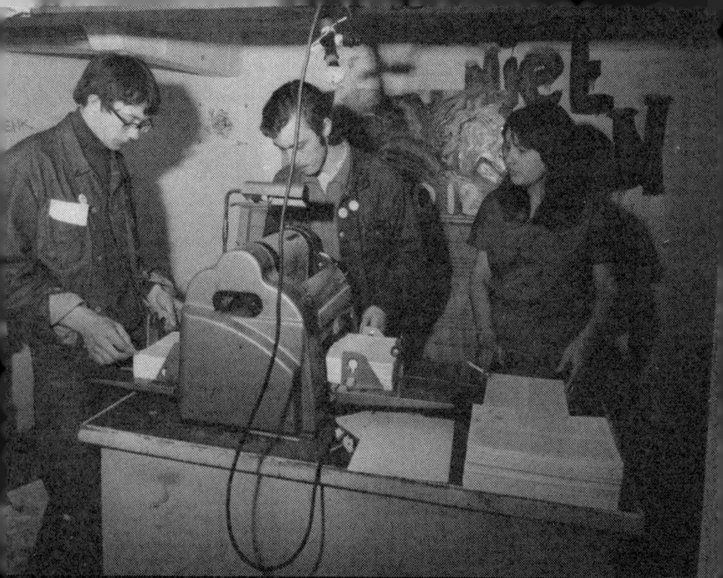

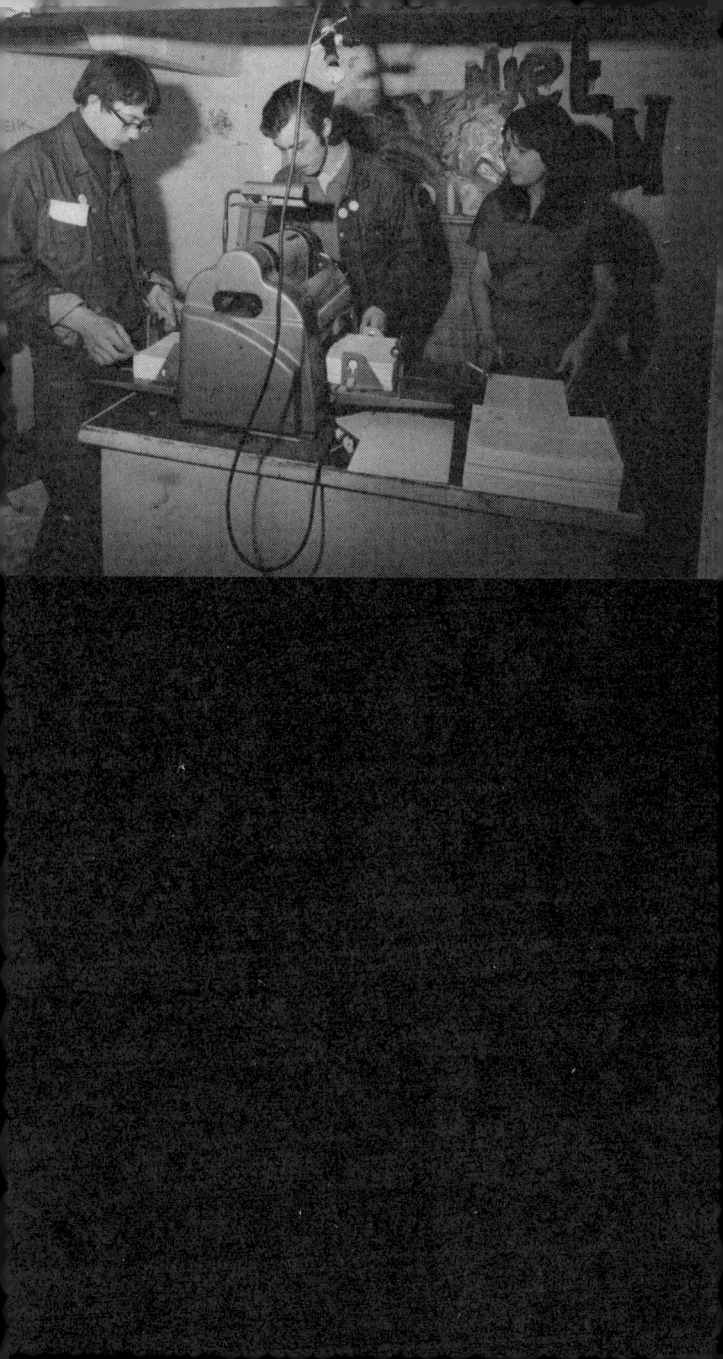

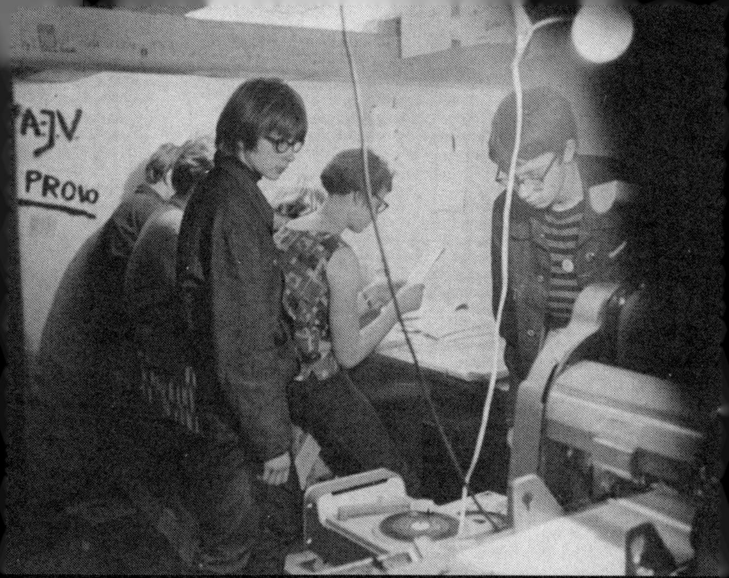

A-J.V
PROW

s. De 'provocatie' die gegooid werd in de boot waarin Be
s op 3 juli 1965 door de Amsterdamse grachten voeren.
Demonstrant tijdens het huwelijk van Beatrix en C

wij zijn
niet
ORANJE
BESMET !

lje
ter
ij,
in.

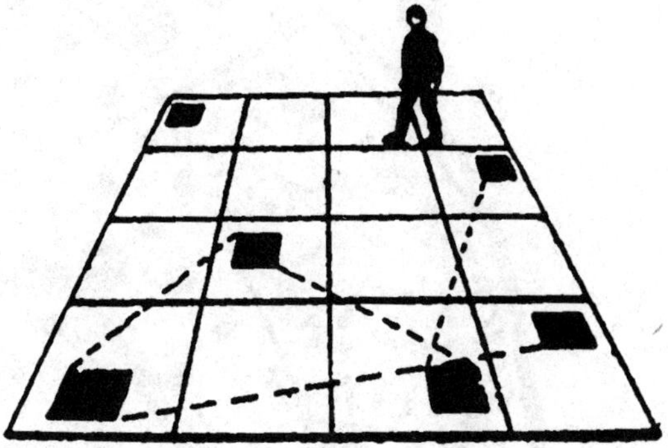

Fig. 5

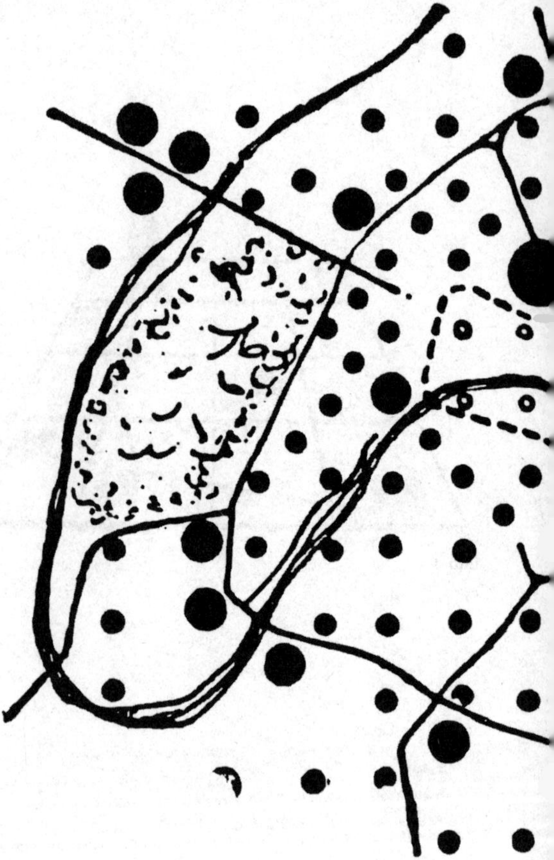

Le progrès

Dans le projet de «
Deryng, « le park

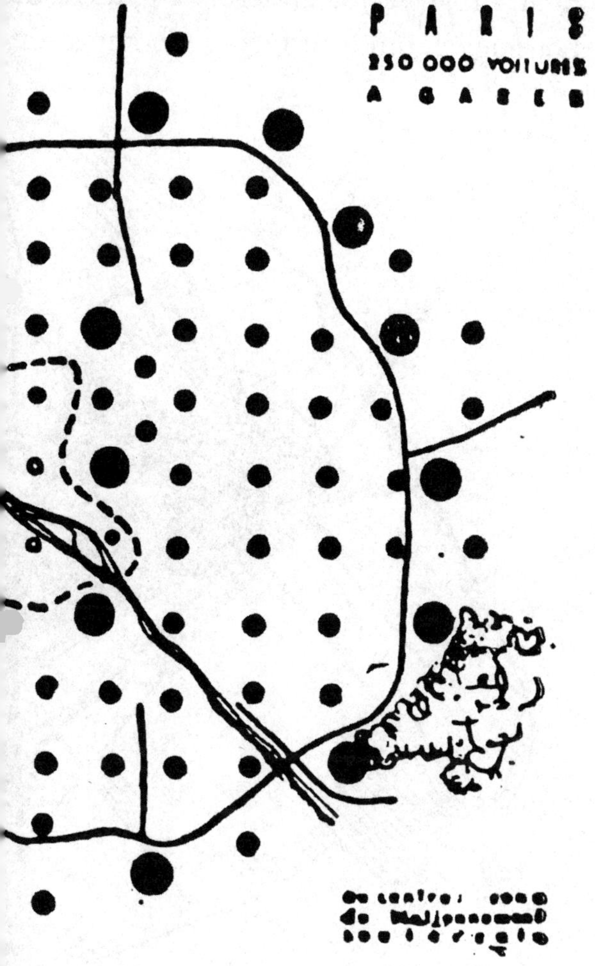

e la maladie.

rage-noyau » de Januz
g commande l'urba-

it les villes autour des

in an urban sector underlies a familiar fra
housing." From Paul-Henry Chombart de

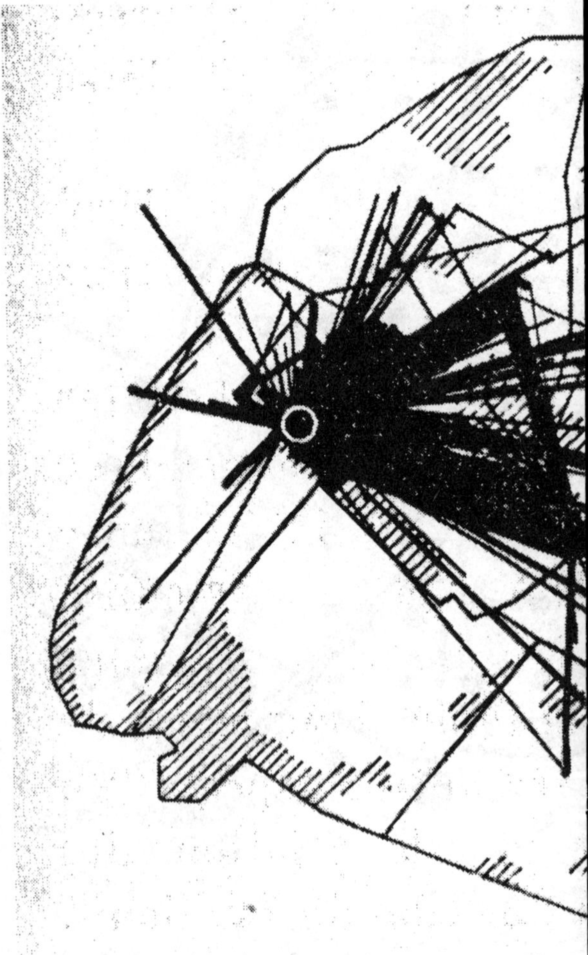

Fig.3.4.4 "Commutes during the cour
The central triangle has for vertices: home
From Paul-Henry Chombart de Lauwe,

rk that exceeds the narrow dimensions of
e, *Paris and the Parisian Region*, 1952.

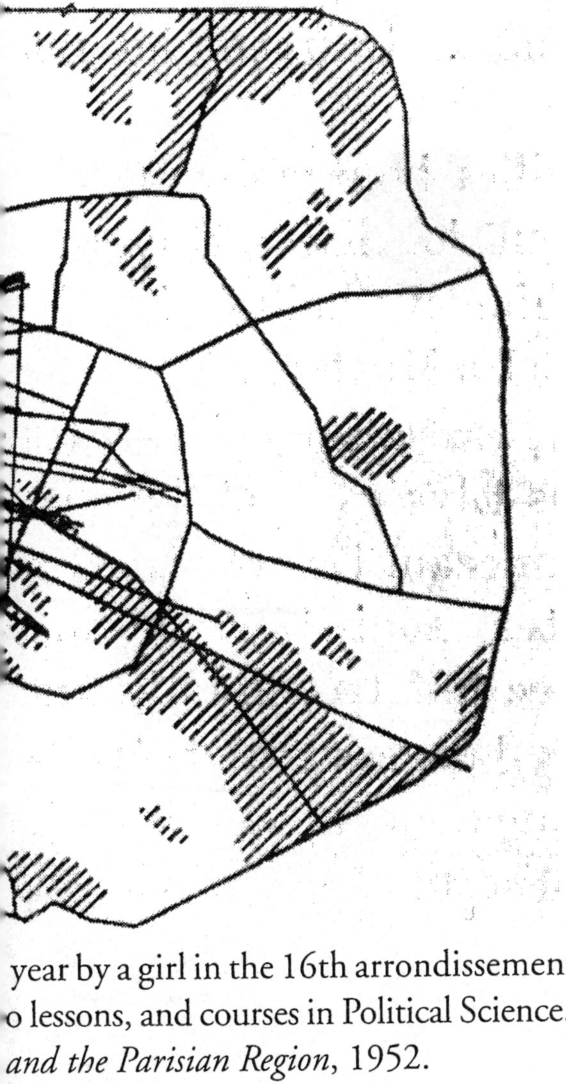

year by a girl in the 16th arrondissement.
o lessons, and courses in Political Science."
and the Parisian Region, 1952.

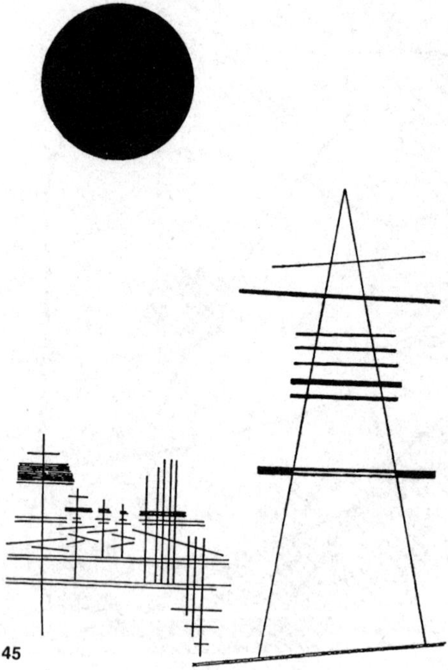

45

5

INTERNAL STRUCTURE OF THE CRAZIES ORGANIZATION

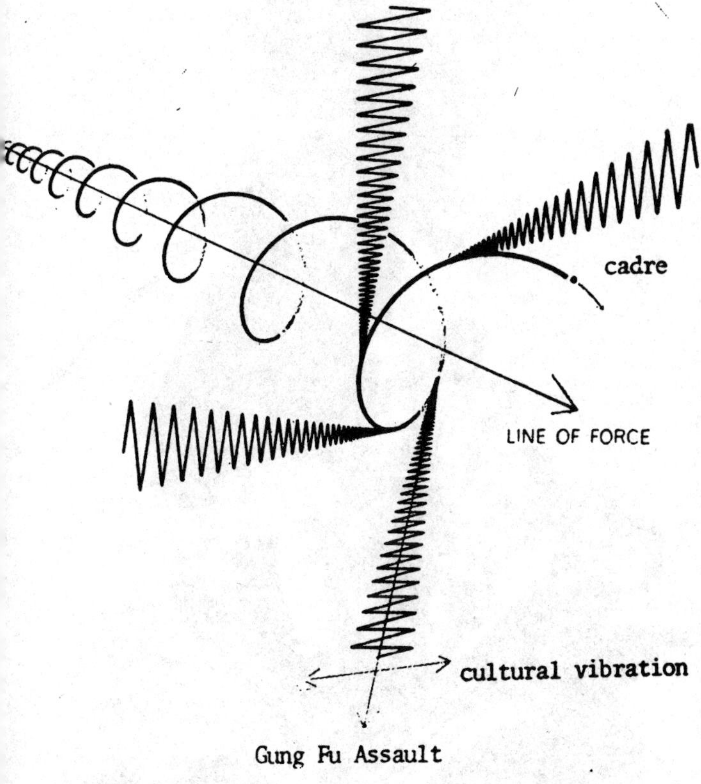

№ 3
новый
леф

Chapter 3

De-con-structions and Re-con-structions

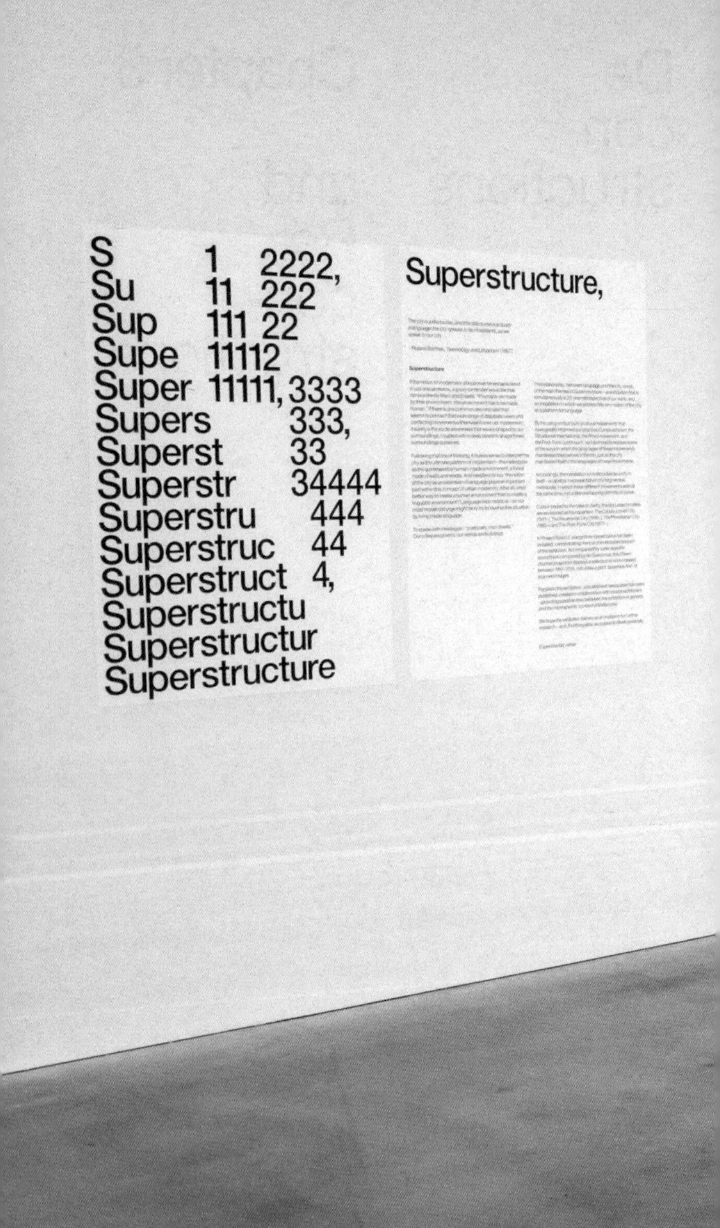
S 1 2222,
Su 11 222
Sup 111 22
Supe 11112
Super 11111, 3333
Supers 333,
Superst 33
Superstr 34444
Superstru 444
Superstruc 44
Superstruct 4,
Superstructu
Superstructur
Superstructure
Superstructure,

THE NAKED CITY
ILLUSTRATION DE L'HYPOTHÈSE DES PLAQUES
TOURNANTES EN PSYCHOGÉOGRAPHIQUE

npapier van De
an een vracht
THE NAKED CITY
INTERNATIONALE SITUATIONNISTE

CHELSEA
our
such a program. We
ed the slightest
secretly slipping SI partisans
only to read us to realise that we
est in such goals and do not use such
The fact is that a few Strasbourg students came
to us in the summer of 1966 and informed us
that six of their friends - and not they them-
of

Een rol krantenpapier van De
Telegraaf is van een vracht

The Situationist
City,
CHELSEA
HIGH RISE LIVING

Een rol krantenpapier van
Telegraaf is van een

Post-Punk

Bakov – 1922 "Concert pour sirènes d'usines et
dans la galerie Barbazanges : la musique
l'ameublement permanent de la salle, à la
lier. Trois brefs morceaux sont joués
musiciens au nombre de 23. Aujourd'hui
aisément renoncer à la répétition constante par
Nous enregistrerons séparément les trois
diffuseront grâce à des bandes
répétées, comme la musique de supermarché,
d'atelier. En 1920, comme les gens
Erik Satie, en colère, se mit à parcourir la
"N'écoutez pas! Circulez! Parlez entre vous!"
Trente-cinq ans plus tard, en 1952, John Cage
compositions majeures du XXe siècle : "4'33".

Bakou – 1922 "Concert pour sirènes d'usines et sifflements de fumée
ent sur le toit d'un grand immeuble
dans la galerie Barbazanges : la musique devait faire partie
l'ameublement permanent de la salle, à la manière du mo
lier. Trois brefs morceaux sont joués parallèlement par d
musiciens au nombre de 23. Aujourd'hui nous pouvo
aisément renoncer à la répétition constante par des musicie
Nous enregistrerons séparément les trois morceaux et
diffuseront grâce à des bandes magnétiques indéfinim
répétées, comme la musique de supermarché, d'aéroport
d'atelier. En 1920, comme les gens écoutaient en silen
Erik Satie, en colère, se mit à parcourir la galerie en crian
"N'écoutez pas! Circulez! Parlez entre vous!"
Trente-cinq ans plus tard, en 1952, John Cage publia une d
compositions majeures du XXe siècle : "4'33".
dor créa l'œuvre : il était assis au piano
les bras pour indiquer que le morceau
Cage déclara que les bruits que
pendant ce temps étaient sa musique.
John Cage, qui était professeur au
développa le prototype du Happe-
ient réduits au minimum. Chaque
partition où figurait seulement
il avait le libre choix de faire ce
Cage fit un exposé sur le
le bouddhisme zen rien n'est bien
ne doit être rien d'autre que
mme la vie, rempli de hasards..."
19

Der Neue Luxus
De Nieuwe Luxe
Le Luxe Nouveau
naim/ bureau europa
The New Luxury
ALISON &PETER SMITHSON:
naim/ bureau europa
THE ART INHABITATION OF
ALISON &PETER SMITHSON:
17.12.2011–2
ART THE OF INHABITATION
www.bureau-europa.nl
NAiM / Bureau Europa
Avenue Céramique
Maastricht

The Post-Punk
4444444
444444
44444
4444
444
44
4

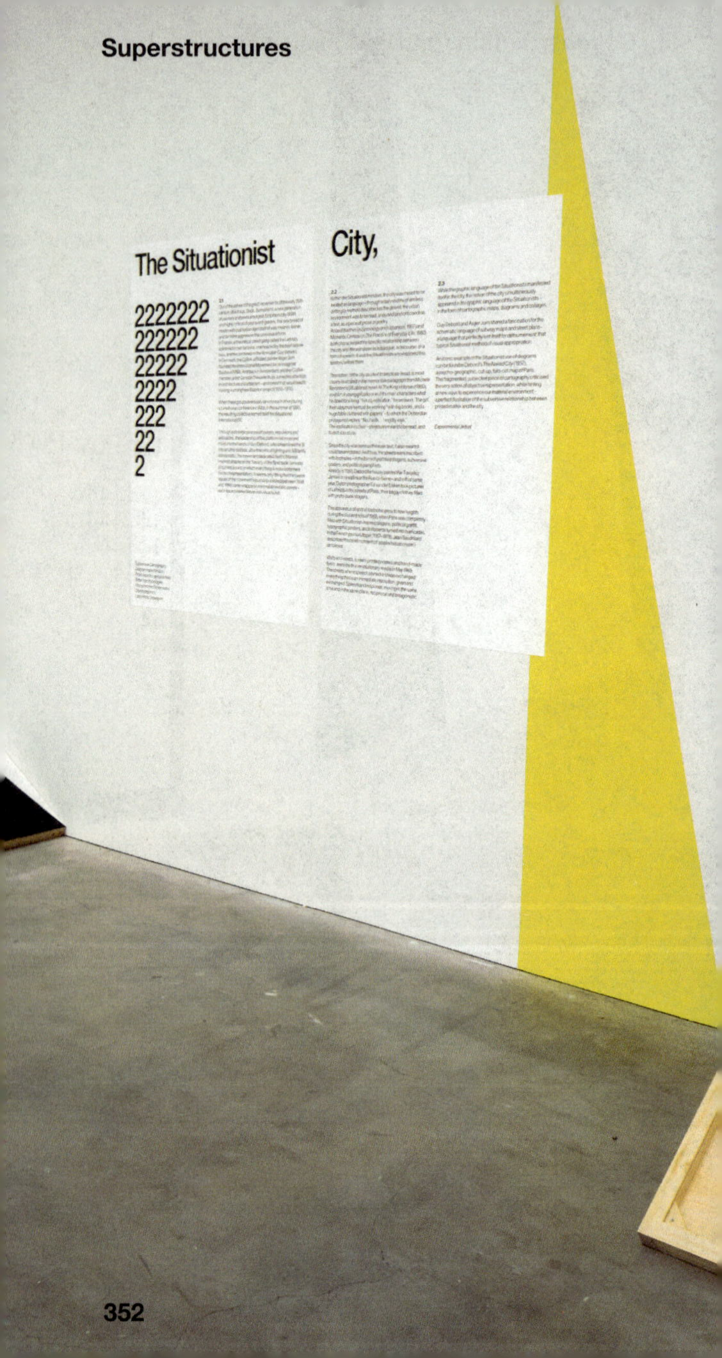
The Situationist
City,
2222222
222222
22222
2222
222
22
2

The Provotarian
City,
3333333
333333
33333
3333
333
33
3

MAGE
Il monumento di Tatlin è alto, nel
bozzetto, circa 25 metri, ma il progetto

MERDE
PROVO
HOMO-SEX
which would be a rallying point thr
Bier

PROVO 12
ANARCHIE
JOOP
NE TRAVAILLE
JAM
ppen.
to s

PROVO 12
ANARCHIE

City,
PIL

TUXEDOMOON
PERE UBU

The Post-Punk
City,
4444444
444444
44444
4444
444
44
4

Een rol krantenpapier van De
Telegraaf is van een vracht

IMAGE

City,

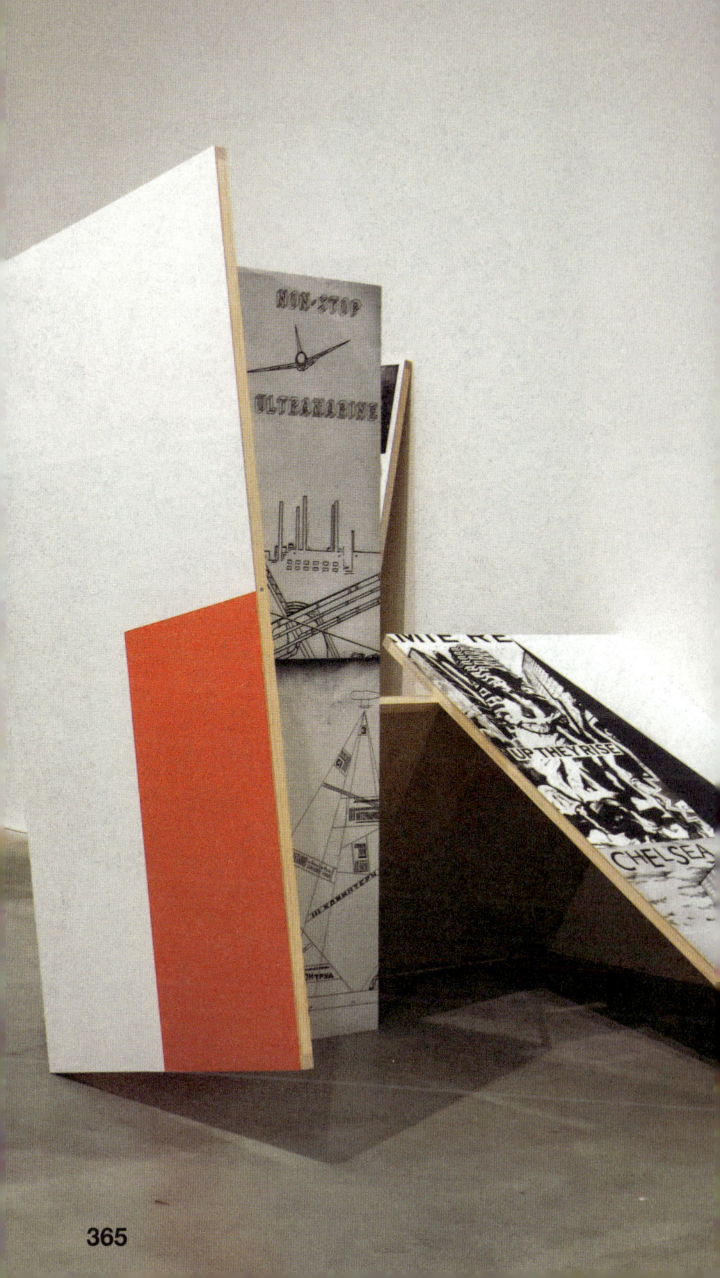
NON-STOP
ULTRAMARINE
UP THEY RISE
CHELSEA

PIL
Chaos
Atom
Poesie
Cut
Cover
Afrika
Privat
Club

NU EN HIER
H.M.VAN RANDWYK

The Constructivist
City,

evich, Suprematistische wolkenkrabber, 1925
domanda e alla loro
on è più determinabil
suo valore d'uso,
1924.

MERDE
PROVO
HOMO-SEX
voil

nous voulons une université populaire
DU PEUPLE
SANEREN-DEPORTEREN
SPECULEREN
goede
sezuan

ECONOMIC ANGST
World of Money
9 April 99
Anarchitecture,
8 June 99
bureau
europa

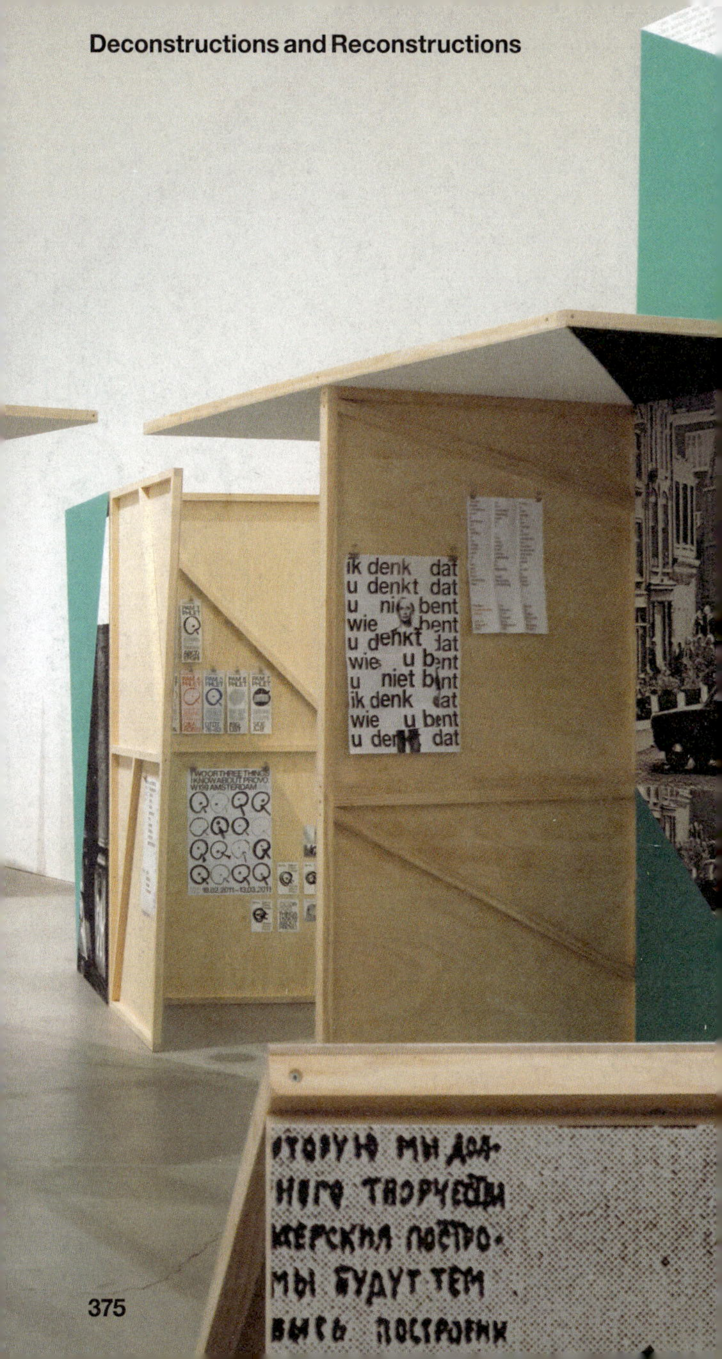
ik denk dat
u denkt dat

binnenstad.
PROVO
PAM 0
PHLET
INTRO
TEXT
PAM 1
PHLET
ABCD
EFGHI
PAM 2
PHLET
Q&A
ROB/1
PAM 3
PHLET
Q&A
SARA
PAM 4
PHLET
Q&A
ROB/2

Melbourne
Superstructure
Brno, Two or Three

3.03.2011
Brno, Two o
Three
Thing
I Know
About
Provo,
Brno, Two or
Three
Things
I Know
About
Provo,
Two or Three Things I Know About Provo
OR
THINGS
I KNOW
ABOUT
PROVO

nieuw soort verschenen overal in de binnenstad.
cties waren 'ludiek' of speels en bevorc
PAM 0 PHLET
INTRO TEXT
PAM 1 PHLET
ABCD EFGHI
PAM 2 PHLET
Q&A ROB/1
PAM 3 PHLET
Q&A SARA
PAM 4 PHLET
Q&A ROB/2
PAM 5 PHLET
DTDT 76–83
PAM 6 PHLET
IISG LIST
PAM 7 PHLET
SIDE A+B
TWO OR THREE THINGS I KNOW ABOUT PROVO. W139 AMSTERDAM
18.02.2011–13.03.2011
THINGS I KNOW ABOUT PROVO
net zo blind als wij

DE EETBARE STAD/THE EDIBLE CITY
NAi M
Bipolis 2007
Food for Thought / Thoughts on Food
Opening De Eetbare Stad
Programma
RSVP
NAi M
vesteda
Bipolis

Deconstructions and Reconstructions
JOURNALE
ZEI-
ZEITUNGEN
Die junge Frau
Neueste

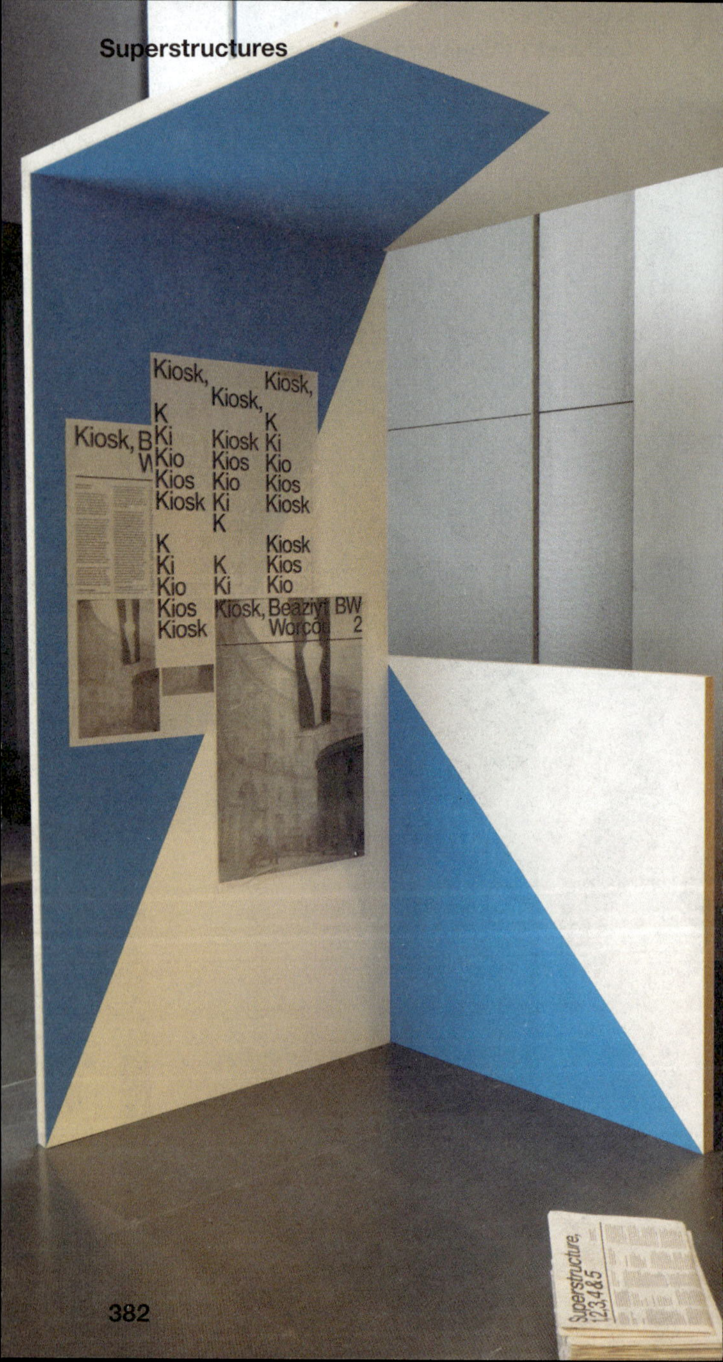
Kiosk,
Kiosk,
Kiosk,
K
Ki
Kio
Kios
Kiosk
Kiosk
Kios
Kio
Ki
K
K
Ki
Kio
Kios
Kiosk
Kiosk
Kios
Kio
K
Ki
BW
2
Superstructure,
1,2,3,4&5

Kiosk,
Kiosk,
Kiosk,
Kiosk
Kiosk
Kios
Kiosk,
Kio
Ki
K
Kios
Kios
Kio
Ki
K

Kiosk,
Kiosk,
Kiosk,
K
Ki
Kio
Kios
Kiosk
Kiosk
Kios
Kio
Ki
K
K
Ki
Kio
Kios
Kiosk
Kiosk
Kios
Kio
K
Ki
Kio
Kios
Kiosk
K
Ki
Kiosk,

Superstructure,
1,2,3,4 & 5

Kiosk, Warren Taylor WT 1
I CAN'T STOP IT
Kiosk, Stuart Geddes SG 1

Worcou
Lumsden-Barry 2
Kiosk
ZT 1
Grocott
Superstructure, low-tech/hi-tech
Žiga Testen
PMF 2
Lisa Grocott LG 1
2018

ARCH
ITECT
URES
TYPO
GRAPH
IQUES
WIM
CROU
WEL

DOES A
LION STOP
Artimo
/kunstenaars
boeken
/kunsttheorie
Artimobij
Marres
/fotografie

THE ATHENS RECORDER

e
S re
Su ure
Sup ture
Supe cture
Super ucture
Supers ructure
Superstructure
Superstr
Superstru
Superstruc
Superstruct
Superstructu
Superstructur
Superstructure
Experimental Jetset–
Superstructure
Tuesday–Friday
10am–5pm
16 March–5 May
Saturday 12–5pm

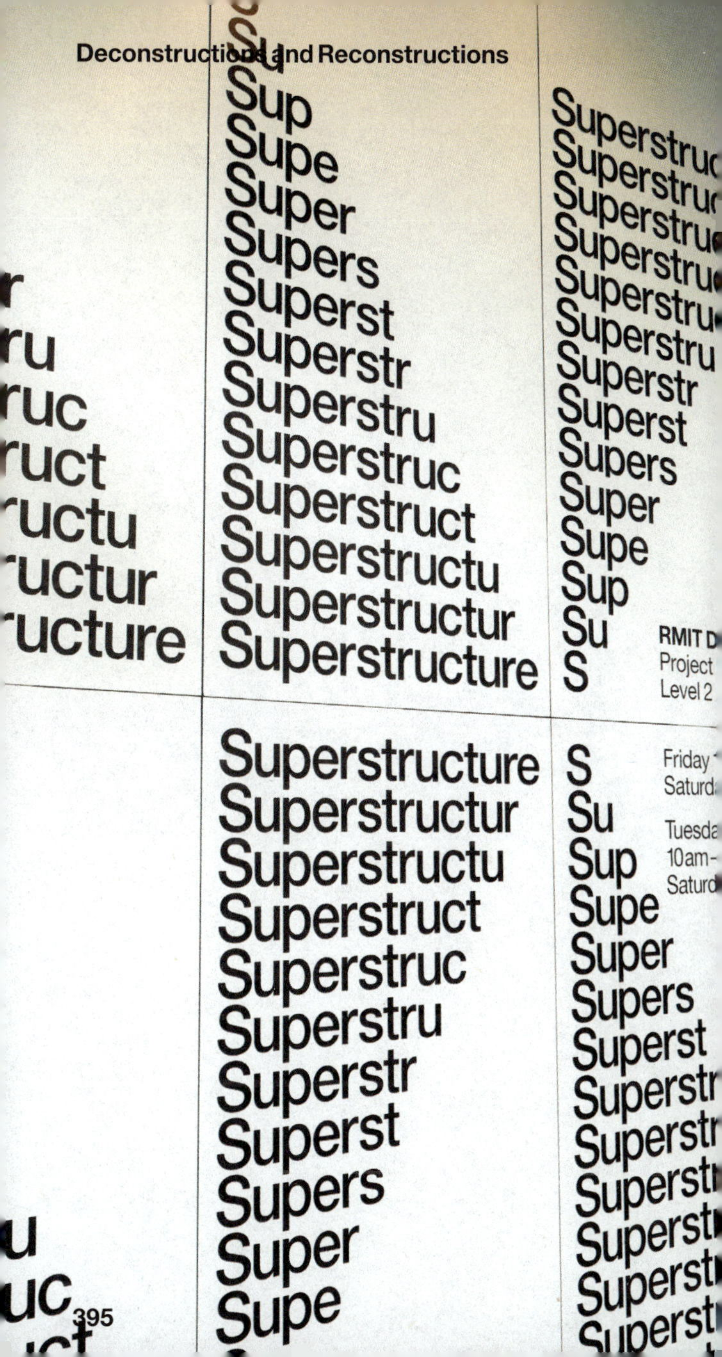
Sup
Supe
Super
Supers
Superst
Superstr
Superstru
Superstruc
Superstruct
Superstructu
Superstructur
Superstructure
ru
ruc
ruct
uctu
uctur
ucture
Superstru
Superstr
Superst
Supers
Super
Supe
Sup
Su
S
RMIT D
Project
Level 2
Superstructure
Superstructur
Superstructu
Superstruct
Superstruc
Superstru
Superstr
Superst
Supers
Super
Supe
S
Su
Sup
Supe
Super
Supers
Superst
Friday
Tuesda
10am–

Appendix

Image credits:

Chapter 2

The Constructivist City,
The Situationist City,
The Provotarian City,
The Post-Punk City

104–107
Barricades in Paris, May 1968
from: Charles Jencks, *Architecture 2000 – Predictions and Methods* (London: Studio Vista, 1971)
Photo: Agip

108–109
Barricades in Paris, May 1968
from: *Beneath the Paving Stones – Situationists and the Beach, May 1968* (San Francisco: AK Press / Dark Star, 2001)
Photographer unknown

110–111
Reclaim the Streets occupation, London, 1995
Photo: Nick Cobbing

112–113
Car Free protests, Amsterdam, 1970s
Photographer unknown

114–115
Provo protest against a ban on protests, Amsterdam, 1966
from: *Delta. A Review of Arts, Life and Thought in the Netherlands. Autumn 1967* (Amsterdam: Delta, 1967)
Photo: Jacques Klok

116–119
Provo protest against a ban on protests, Amsterdam, 1966
Photographer unknown

120–121
Performance, "Parades and Changes" by San Francisco Dancers' Workshop / Anna Halprin, Fresno, CA, 1967
from: Lawrence Halprin, *The RSVP Cycles* (New York: George Braziller, 1969)
Photo: Connie Beeson

122–123
Performance, "Seven Ballets in Manhattan" by Daniel Buren, New York, 1975
Photo: Daniel Buren / Adagp, Paris

124–129
De Telegraaf riots, Amsterdam, 1966
Newspaper clipping, June 14, 1966
Photographer unknown

130–131
Provadya manifestation, Alkmaar, 1970
Photographer unknown

132–133
Performance, "Walk Talk" by Ferdinand Kriwet, 1969
from: Ferdinand Kriwet, *Kriwet Publit* (San Francisco: Nova Broadcast Press, 1971)
Photo: Hans Offergeld

134–135
Performance, "Shadow Project" by Mass Moving, Hiroshima, 1972
Photographer unknown

136–137
Billboard barricade, Paris, 1968
from: Tom McDonough, *The Beautiful Language of My Century, Reinventing the Language of Contestation in Postwar France, 1945–1968* (Cambridge, MA: October Books, MIT Press, 2007)
Photo: Bruno Barbey

138–139
Cover, "Artists' Brigade" no. 4, 1931
from: Wim Beeren, *De Grote Utopie, de Russische Avant-Garde 1915–1932* (Amsterdam: Stedelijk Museum,1992)

140–141
Performance by Blue Blouse, Moscow, 1929
Photographer unknown

142–143
Photo, "New Moscow" by Boris Ignatovich, 1931
from: Wim Beeren, *De Grote Utopie, de Russische Avant-Garde 1915–1932* (Amsterdam: Stedelijk Museum,1992)

144–145
Towards Place de la Bastille, Paris, May 1968
from: *Mai 68 ou l'imagination au pouvoir* (Vence: Galerie Beaubourg / Paris: éditions de la difference,1998)
Photo: Bruno Barbey

146–147
Poster, Crash Happening by Bart Hughes et al., Amsterdam, 1965
from: *Actie, werkelijkheid en fictie in de kunst van de jaren '60 in Nederland* (The Hague: Staatsuitgeverij, 1979)

148–149
Poster wall, École de Beaux-Arts, Paris, June 1968
from: *Mai 68 ou l'imagination au pouvoir* (Vence: Galerie Beaubourg / Paris: éditions de la difference, 1998)
Photo: Bruno Barbey

150–151
Poster, Saneren, Deporteren, Speculeren, Amsterdam, 1972
from: Bas Roodnat, *Wij zijn gek, Nederlandse straatkunst in de jaren zeventig* (Amsterdam: Erven Thomas Rap, 1977)
Photo: Rob Croes

152
Poster, Renovation, Deportation, Speculation, Paris, 1969
from: Johan Kugelberg, Philippe Vermes (eds.), *Beauty is in the Street, A Visual Record of the May '68 Paris Uprising* (London: Four Corner Books, 2011)

154–155
Poster, Action Committees, Paris, 1969
from: Johan Kugelberg, Philippe Vermes (eds.), *Beauty Is in the Street, A Visual Record of the May '68 Paris Uprising* (London: Four Corner Books, 2011)

156–157
Map of Amsterdam (with the area between Emmaplein, Europaplein, Oosterpark,

Nieuwmarkt and bus station removed) by Sol LeWitt, 1976
from: Christophe Cherix, *In & Out of Amsterdam: Travels in Contemporary Art, 1960–1976* (New York: MoMA, 2009)

158–159
"The Naked City" by Guy Debord, 1957
from: Zweifel, Steiner, Stahlhut (eds.), *In Girum Imus Nocte et Consumimur Igni – The Situationist International (1957–1972)* (Zurich: JRP / Ringier Kunstverlag AG / Basel: Museum Tinguely, 2006)

160–161
Barricades map, Paris, Friday, May 10, 1968
from: *L'evenement, Premiere historie de la revolution de Mai* (Paris: L'evenement, 1968)

162–163
Map of October 10, 1980
from: Zwartboekgroep Metrodemonstratie, *De metro demonstratie en hoe 't gezag er 'n rel van maakte* (Amsterdam: Uitgeverij Lont, 1980)

164
Cover, "Pamphlets in May 68"
from: Michel Demonet, *Des tracts en mai 68* (Paris: Fondation nationale des sciences politiques / Armand Colin, 1975)

165
"The Wall" by Paul Armand Gette, 1968
from: Steef Davidson, *Images de la Revolte 1965–1975* (Paris: Editions Henri Feyrier, 1982)

166–169
Tatlin's Tower, 1925
from: Apollonio, Caramel, Mahlow, *Ricerca e progettazione, proposte per una esposizione sperimentale* (Venice: la Biennale di Venezia, 1970)

170–171
Tatlin's Tower, 1919/1920
from: Apollonio, Caramel, Mahlow, *Ricerca e progettazione, proposte per una esposizione sperimentale* (Venice: la Biennale di Venezia, 1970)

172–173
Provo headquarters in the former Apollo cinema, Amsterdam, 1967
Archive of the Department of City Planning Amsterdam
Photographer unknown

174–175
Provo graffiti, Orange Provo / Pill, Amsterdam, 1960s
from: Richter Roegholt, *Amsterdam in de 20e eeuw 2 (1945–1970)* (Utrecht / Antwerp: Het Spectrum, 1979)

176–177
March by Dutch feminist group Dolle Mina to promote the birth control pill, ca. 1970
from: Christophe Cherix, *In & Out of Amsterdam: Travels in Contemporary Art, 1960–1976* (New York: MoMA, 2009)

178–179
Protest against air pollution, Amsterdam, 1970
from: Bert Bommels, Evert

Werkman, *Je blijft lachen in Amsterdam* (Amsterdam: Het Parool, 1971)

180–181
Carnival procession by Heinz Mack, Otto Piene, and Günther Uecker, Düsseldorf, February 10, 1964
from: Pörschmann, Schavemaker (eds.), *Zero* (Amsterdam: Stedelijk Museum / Düsseldorf: Zero Foundation / Cologne: Walther Köning, 2015)

182–185
Performance, "Towards Thee Crystal Bowl" by Cosey Fanni Tutti and Genesis P-Orridge, Milan, 1976
from: Simon Ford, *Wreckers of Civilisation: The Story of Coum Transmissions & Throbbing Gristle* (London: Black Dog Publishing, 1999)

186
Provoos in New Babylon, Provo no. 4, 1965
from: *Actie, werkelijkheid en fictie in de kunst van de jaren '60 in Nederland* (The Hague: Staatsuitgeverij, 1979)

188–189
"Ladder-Labyrinth" by Constant, 1967
from: Simon Sadler, *The Situationist City* (Cambridge, MA / London: MIT Press, 1998)

190–191
Performance, "Parades and Changes" by San Francisco Dancers' Workshop / Anna Halprin, Fresno, CA, 1967
from: Lawrence Halprin, *The RSVP Cycles* (New York: George Braziller, 1969)
Photo: Larry Goldsmith

192
Squatting action, Amsterdam, 1970s
Photographer unknown

193
Squatting action, Amsterdam, 1970s
Photographer unknown

194
Graffiti, Bureau IJtunnel, Amsterdam, 1970s
from: *Even geduld deze straat is gekraakt* (Amsterdam: Uitgeverij Lont, 1980)

195
Squatting action, Amsterdam, 1980s
Photographer unknown

197
Graffiti, Image / Paradise Now, Amsterdam, 1970s
from: Bas Roodnat, *Wij zijn gek, Nederlandse straatkunst in de jaren zeventig* (Amsterdam: Erven Thomas Rap, 1977)
Photo: Rob Croes

198–199
Inscription on a wall, Rue de Seine, 1953, Internationale Situationniste no. 8, 1963
from: Greil Marcus, *Lipstick Traces* (London: Secker & Warburg, 1989)

201
Wall rubbing by Experimental Jetset (2014), of a Gnot sign

engraved by Robert Jasper Grootveld on the Palace at Dam Square, 1965
from: Johannes Schwartz *High Signs* (Amsterdam: Schwartz, 2014)

202–203
Provo banner, "Provo Image"
from: Roel van Duijn (ed.), *Provo, de Geschiedenis van De Provotarische Beweging 1965–1967* (Amsterdam: Meulenhoff, 1985)
Photo: Cor Jaring

204–205
Graffiti, Provo Image on the Van Heutsz monument, 1965
from: *Het Vrije Volk*, 1965

206–207
Graffiti, Provo 12, Amsterdam
from: Bas Roodnat, *Wij zijn gek, Nederlandse straatkunst in de jaren zeventig* (Amsterdam: Erven Thomas Rap, 1977)

208
Graffiti, Provo 12, Amsterdam
from: *Goed Wonen* no. 9, (Amsterdam: Stichting Goed Wonen, 1966)
Photo: Johan van der Keuken

210–211
Suprematist skyscraper by Kazimir Malevich, 1925
from: Wim Beeren, *De Grote Utopie, de Russische Avant-Garde 1915–1932* (Amsterdam: Stedelijk Museum, 1992)

212–213
Nieuwmarkt "Color Project," Amsterdam, 1970s
from: Bas Roodnat, *Wij zijn gek, Nederlandse straatkunst in de jaren zeventig* (Amsterdam: Erven Thomas Rap, 1977)

214
Nieuwmarkt evictions, Amsterdam, 1975
from: Van Lakerveld, Smiers (eds.), *Matheid, hoezo?* (Amsterdam: Sjaloom, 1981)
Photo: Pieter Boersma

216–217
Record sleeve, Killing Joke, by Michael Coles, 1980
from: *Killing Joke* (London: E.G. Records, 1980)

219
Critique of Urbanism
from: *Internationale Situationniste* no. 10 (Paris: IS, March 1966)

220–221
Paris, May 1968
from: *Beneath the Paving Stones – Situationists and the Beach, May 1968* (San Francisco: AK Press / Dark Star, 2001)

222–223
Provo smoke bombs by Peter Bronkhorst (l) and Rob Stolk (r), Amsterdam, 1966
Photo: Cor Jaring

224–227
Provo smoke signals, Amsterdam, 1966
from: Roel van Duijn (ed.), *Provo, de Geschiedenis van De Provotarische Beweging 1965–1967* (Amsterdam: Meulenhoff, 1985)
Photo: Cor Jaring

228–231
Concert for factory sirens and steam whistles, "Symphony of Sirens" by Arseny Avraamov, Moscow, 1923
from: Suzanne Pagé, *Écouter par les yeux* (Paris: ARC / Musée d'Art Moderne de la Ville de Paris, 1980)

232–233
Provo happening at the Spui, Amsterdam, April 1967
from: Elsevier Photo Archive

234
Provo happening with Rob Stolk and Robert Jasper Grootveld, Amsterdam, August 1965
from: Elsevier Photo Archive
Photo: Ab Pruis

235
Provo happening, Amsterdam
from: Huub Schoondergang, *En toen kwamen de kabouters* (Leiden: A.W. Sijthoff, 1971)

236–237
Provo happening at the Spui, Amsterdam, 1966
from: Christophe Cherix, *In & Out of Amsterdam: Travels in Contemporary Art, 1960–1976* (New York: MoMA, 2009)

238–239
Situationists throwing their pamphlets from the window [...] where they have installed the committee of the occupation of the Sorbonne, Paris, 1968
from: Laurent Chollet, *L'insurrection Situationniste* (Paris: Editions Dagorno, 2000)

240
Performance, "Danger Music no. 2" by Dick Higgins and Alison Knowles at Fluxus Internationale Festspiele Neuester Musik, Wiesbaden, 1962
Photo: Hartmut Rekort

242–243
Model for a skyscaper at Potsdamer Platz by Erich Buchholz, 1921

244–245
Exhibition of students' work on the revelation and expression of mass and weight, Vkhutemas, 1927–1928
from: The Archive of the Schusev State Museum of Architecture, Moscow, Russia

246
Study of vertical rhythm, exercise on volumetric composition, Vkhutemas workshop, 1920–1926
from: Witkovsky, Fore (eds.), *Revoliutsiia! Demonstratsiia! Soviet Art Put to the Test* (Chicago: The Art Institute of Chicago, 2017)

247
"Tyrannical Tower" by Eduardo Paolozzi, 1961

248
Skyscraper sketches by Erich Mendelsohn, 1922

249
Sketch for a railway station by Hans Scharoun, 1922

250–251
Drawing by Malcolm McLaren, October 1969
from: Jon Savage, *England's Dreaming* (New York: St. Martin's Press, 2002)

252
Futuristic pavilion at the World's Fair by Enrico Prampolini, Turin, 1928
from: Theo van Doesburg, *De Stijl en de Europese architectuur: de architectuuropstellen in Het Bouwbedrijf 1924–1931* (Nijmegen: SUN, 1986)

253
Book Pavilion by Fortunato Depero, Monza Biennale, Milan, 1927
from: Ferdinand Kriwet, *Kriwet Publit* (San Francisco: Nova Broadcast Press, 1971)
Photo: Hans Offergeld

254
Pavilion at the All-Russia Agricultural Exhibition by Alexandra Exter, Vera Mukhina, and Boris Gladkov, Moscow, 1923
from: Wim Beeren, *De Grote Utopie, de Russische Avant-Garde 1915–1932* (Amsterdam: Stedelijk Museum, 1992)

255
Lenin Tribune by El Lissitzky, Moscow, 1920
from: The Collection of State Tretyakov Gallery, Moscow

256–257
UNOVIS, November 20, 1920
from: Wim Beeren, *De Grote Utopie, de Russische Avant-Garde 1915–1932* (Amsterdam: Stedelijk Museum, 1992)

258
Design for a kiosk by Alexander Rodchenko, 1919
from: Szymon Bojko, *New Graphic Design in Revolutionary Russia* (New York: Praeger, 1972)

259
Design for "Loudspeaker no. 3" by G.G. Klucis, 1922
from: Margaret Rowell, Angelica Zander Rudenstine, *Art of the Avant-Garde in Russia: Selections from the George Costakis Collection* (New York: The Solomon R. Guggenheim Foundation, 1981)

260–261
Record sleeve, "Non-stop / Ultramarine," WKGB, 1980
from: Tony Brook, Adrian Shaughnessy (eds.), *Action Time Vision* (London: Unit Editions, 2016)

262–263
"Sketch of the Installation for the Mass Action at Khodynka Field" by Liubov Popova, 1921
from: Witkovsky, Fore (eds.) *Revoliutsiia! Demonstratsiia! Soviet Art Put to the Test* (Chicago: The Art Institute of Chicago, 2017)

264
"Capsule Homes Tower" by Warren Chalk, 1964
from: Michael Franklin Ross, *Beyond Metabolism* (New York: Architectural Record, 1978)

265
"Kibogaoka Youth Castle" by Tatsuhiko Nakajima and GAUS, Kyoto, Japan, 1972
from: Michael Franklin Ross, *Beyond Metabolism* (New York: Architectural Record, 1978)

266
Design for a city apartment building in concrete by Georg Muche, 1924
from: Hans M. Wingler, *The Bauhaus* (Cambridge, MA: MIT Press, 1969)

267
Record sleeve, "High Rise Living / No Admission," Chelsea, 1977
from: Tony Brook, Adrian Shaughnessy (eds.), *Action Time Vision* (London: Unit Editions, 2016)

268–269
Record sleeve, "Dub Housing," Pere Ubu, 1978
from: LP, *Dub Housing* (New York: Chrysalis Records, 1978)

270–271
Record sleeve, "Scream with a View," Tuxedo Moon, 1979
from: EP, *Scream with a View* (San Francisco: Tuxedomoon, 1979)

273
Collage, "Science Holiday" by Skot Armstrong, 1977
from: Johan Kugelberg, John Savage (eds.), *Punk, an Aesthetic* (New York: Rizzoli, 2012)

274
Zine, "City Fun" no. 11, 1979
from: Manchester Digital Music Archive (Manchester: Grass Roots, November 6, 1979)

276
Record sleeve, "This Is the Modern World," The Jam, 1977
from: LP, *This Is the Modern World* (London: Polydor, 1977)

278–279
Book cover, "Up They Rise" by Jamie Reid, 1987
from: Jamie Reid, John Savage, *Up They Rise: The Incomplete Works of Jamie Reid* (London: Faber & Faber Limited, 1987)

280
"4) and our [collective] home"
from: Rosta Window poster no. 160, Moscow, ca. 1920

281–282
Apartment interior at the Weissenhofsiedlung by Ludwig Mies van der Rohe and Lilly Reich, Stuttgart, 1927
from: Theo van Doesburg, *De Stijl en de Europese architectuur: De architectuuropstellen in Het Bouwbedrijf 1924–1931* (Nijmegen: SUN, 1986)

283
"Cabinet of Abstraction" by El Lissitzky, Museum Hannover, 1927

284
Models for prefabricated houses by Walter Gropius and Hannes Meyer, 1923

from: Hans M. Wingler, *The Bauhaus* (Cambridge, MA: MIT Press, 1969)

285
Typology of minimum wage housing by A. Klein, 1929
from: Manfredo Tafuri, *Ontwerp en Utopie* (Nijmegen: SUN, 1978)

287
Amsterdam City Center, Paris Montmartre, Amsterdam Rivierenbuurt, 1950s
from: Martin van Schaik, Otakar Mačel, *Exit Utopia, Architectural Provocations 1956–76* (Delft: IHAAU-TU Delft / Munich: Prestel, 2005)

288–289
Project for a high-rise city by Ludwig Karl Hilberseimer, 1924
from: Hans M. Wingler, *The Bauhaus* (Cambridge, MA: MIT Press, 1969)

290–291
Damage, October 1980
(San Francisco: Damaged Goods Co., 1979–1981)

292–293
Constructing the set of the City of the Future for "Metropolis," 1927
from: Friedrich-Wilhelm-Murnau Stiftung, Photo: Horst von Harbou

295
Schematic survey of the field of instruction "Man" by Oskar Schlemmer, 1928–1929
from: Hans M. Wingler, *The Bauhaus* (Cambridge, MA: MIT Press, 1969)

296–298
Book Bloc, London, December 2010
Photographer unknown

299
Citroën workers on strike, May 29, 1968
Photographer unknown

300–301
Rhodiaceta textile factory workers on strike, Besançon, May 1968
Photographer unknown

302–303
Living Newspaper by Blue Blouse, Moscow, 1920s
Photographer unknown

304–305
Printing pamphlets in the occupied Maagdenhuis by ex-Provo Rob Stolk and students, Amsterdam, May 1969
Photographer unknown

306–307
Pamphlets for the radio station of the occupied Maagdenhuis by Rob Stolk, Amsterdam, May 1969
Photographer unknown

308
Sunday morning, March 2, 1980
from: *Even geduld deze straat is gekraakt* (Amsterdam: Uitgeverij Lont,1980)
Photographer unknown

309
Crash Happening by Bart Hughes, Amsterdam, 1965
from: *Actie, werkelijkheid en fictie in de kunst van de jaren '60 in Nederland* (The Hague: Staatsuitgeverij, 1979)

310
Slogan, Merde
Photo: Archive Spaarnestad

311
Slogan, Provo / Legalize gay sex, Amsterdam, 1966
from: International Institute for Social History (IISG)
Photo: Cor Jaring

312
Poster, "Le Couple Témoin" by William Klein, 1977

313
"They are poisoning you" by Atelier Populaire, Paris, 1968

314–315
Printing of Provo magazine, Amsterdam, 1966
Photographer unknown

316
Provo pamphlets, March 10, 1965, Amsterdam
from: Hans Righart, *De eindeloze jaren zestig – geschiedenis van een generatieconflict* (Amsterdam: de Arbeiderspers,1995)
Photo: Ed van der Elsken

317
Provo protest sign, "We are contaminated with Orange," and fake moustache by Sara Stolk, Amsterdam, 1966

318
Provo pamphlet hat, "White Bike Plan" by Rob Stolk, 1965
(Amsterdam: Het Parool, September 28, 1965)
Photo: Hans Bruggeman

320
"Figure in Space with Plane Geometry and Spatial Delineations" by Oskar Schlemmer, 1924

321
Symbol of the Social Engineering Laboratory of TsIT (Central Institute of Labor), Moscow, 1924
from: Witkovsky, Fore (eds.), *Revoliutsiia! Demonstratsiia! Soviet Art Put to the Test* (Chicago: The Art Institute of Chicago, 2017)

322–323
Le progrès de la maladie
from: *Internationale Situationniste* no. 9 (Paris: IS, August 1964)

324–325
Commutes during the course of a year by a girl in the 16th arrondissement
from: Tom McDonough (ed.), *The Situationists and the City* (London / New York: Verso Books, 2009)

326
"The thin lines prevail against the heavy dot" by Wassily Kandinsky, 1926
from: Hans M. Wingler, *The Bauhaus* (Cambridge, MA: MIT Press, 1969)

327
"Internal Structure of the Crazies Organization" by Viktor Grebennikov

328
Independence of Algeria, 1962
from: Laurent Chollet, *L'insurrection Situationniste* (Paris: Editions Dagorno, 2000)

329
Cover, "Novi Lef" no. 3 by Alexander Rodchenko, 1923
from: Szymon Bojko, *New Graphic Design in Revolutionary Russia* (New York: Praeger, 1972)

330–331
Deciding where to put the Mayakovsky monument, Moscow, 1956
Photo: Dmitri Baltermants

332
Provo happening at the Domela Nieuwenhuis statue, Amsterdam, ca. 1966
from: International Institute for Social History (IISG)

333
Provo happening at the "Lieverdje" statue, Amsterdam, August 1965
from: International Institute for Social History (IISG)
Photo: Ab Pruis

334
Provo happening at the Domela Nieuwenhuis statue, Amsterdam
from: International Institute for Social History (IISG)
Photo: Ab Pruis

335
Happening by Robert Jasper Grootveld at the "Dokwerker" statue, Amsterdam
from: International Institute for Social History (IISG)
Photo: Ab Pruis

Acknowledgements

Contributors, in alphabetical order:

Vasyl Cherepanyn
is Head of the Visual Culture Research Center (VCRC, Kyiv), and works as a lecturer at the Cultural Studies Department of the University of Kyiv-Mohyla Academy. He recently co-edited *Guidebook of the Kyiv International* (Medusa Books, 2018) and *'68 NOW* (Archive Books, 2019), and curated *The European International* (Rijksakademie van Beeldende Kunsten, Amsterdam) and *Hybrid Peace* (Stroom, The Hague) projects. VCRC is the organizer of *The School of Kyiv – Kyiv Biennial 2015, The Kyiv International – Kyiv Biennial 2017*, and *Black Cloud – Kyiv Biennial 2019*.

Leontine Coelewij
is an art historian and curator of contemporary art at the Stedelijk Museum Amsterdam. Her most recent exhibitions at the Stedelijk Museum are *Marlene Dumas: The Image as Burden*, *Seth Siegelaub: Beyond Conceptual Art*, *Edward Krasinski*, *Amsterdam the Magic Center: Art and Counterculture 1967–1970*, *Nam June Paik – The Future Is Now*, and the upcoming *Bruce Nauman* (2021).

Linda van Deursen
is a graphic designer and teacher based in Amsterdam. She co-founded Mevis & Van Deursen in 1987. Between 2000 and 2014, she served as head of the graphic design department at the Gerrit Rietveld Academie. She is senior critic at Yale School of Art and teaches at the Royal Academy of Art in The Hague.

Experimental Jetset
is a graphic design studio based in Amsterdam, founded in 1997 by Erwin Brinkers, Danny van den Dungen, and Marieke Stolk.

Owen Hatherley
was born in Southampton, England, in 1981. He received a PhD from Birkbeck College in 2011, for the thesis *The Political Aesthetics of Americanism*. He writes regularly on architecture, culture, and politics for a variety of publications, and has published several books: *Militant Modernism* (Zero, 2009), *A Guide to the New Ruins of Great Britain* (Verso, 2010), *Uncommon–An Essay on Pulp* (Zero, 2011), *Across the Plaza* (Strelka, 2012), *A New Kind of Bleak* (Verso, 2012), *Landscapes of Communism* (Penguin, 2015), *The Ministry of Nostalgia* (Verso, 2016), *The Chaplin Machine* (Pluto Press, 2016). *Trans-Europe Express* (Penguin, 2018), and *The Adventures of Owen Hatherley in the Post-Soviet Space* (Repeater, 2018). *Red Metropolis–An Essay on the Government of London* will be published by Repeater in late 2020. He is the culture editor of *Tribune*.

Brad Haylock
is a designer, publisher, and academic who lives and works on the unceded lands of the people of the Woiwurrung and Boonwurrung language groups of the Eastern Kulin Nation. He is an Associate Professor in the School of Design at RMIT University, where he is currently Coordinator of Higher Degrees by Research. He has edited and published numerous books, and has most recently co-edited *One and Many Mirrors: Perspectives on Graphic Design Education* (2020) and *Distributed* (2018). His curatorial projects span art and design, and include major exhibitions of the work of Experimental Jetset and Metahaven.

Dirk van den Heuvel
is an architect and associate professor at TU Delft. He heads the Jaap Bakema Study Centre at Het Nieuwe Instituut in Rotterdam. He authored the books *Habitat: Ecology Thinking in Architecture* (2020) and *Jaap Bakema and the Open Society* (2018). He was a Richard Rogers Fellow at Harvard GSD (2017), and together with

Experimental Jetset and Guus Beumer he curated the Dutch pavilion at the Venice Architecture Biennale (2014).

Lieven Lahaye
is an artist and librarian interested in the value of ephemeral information and amateur practices. He produces printed matter, furniture, and performances. Since 2016, he's written and published *Catalog*, a serial publication about cataloging, designed by Ott Metusala.

Masato Samata (Delaware)
is leader of Japanese multimedia group Delaware. Selected works include *SCRAP* (ceramic art / used vinyl record, 2014), *Breathing, Occasionally Art* (cinema based on HTML, 2018), *One Sound Per Second* (music, 2019), and *NOBODY LOVES YOU* (novel that is fun to not read, 2020).

Tom McDonough
is a writer and critic based in upstate New York and Ottawa. He publishes extensively on contemporary art and is currently Associate Professor of Art History at Binghamton University. His most recent book is the anthology *Boredom* (Whitechapel, 2017).

Kateryna Mishchenko
is a publisher and curator living in Kyiv. She is co-founder of the Ukrainian publishing house Medusa. Her essays have been published in Ukrainian and international journals, anthologies, and in the book *Ukrainian Night* (co-authored with Miron Zownir).

Other Forms
is a mobile research and design collective consisting of Jack Henrie Fisher and Alan Smart, working in multiple intersections of architecture, graphic design, and publishing. Other Forms considers how design reflects and critiques, in semi-autonomous marginal spaces, the material and social conditions of its practice.

Mark Owens
is a graphic designer, writer, publisher, and curator, working between New York, Los Angeles, and Philadelphia. His essays have appeared in *Dot Dot Dot*, *Visible Language*, and *PIN-UP*, and he co-edited *Forms of Inquiry* (2007). A book-length study, *Graphics Incognito*, is forthcoming.

Megan Patty
is Head of Publications, Photographic Services and Library at the National Gallery of Victoria, Melbourne, Australia, and is founding Curator of the Melbourne Art Book Fair. She lives and works on the unceded lands of the people of the Woiwurrung and Boonwurrung language groups of the Eastern Kulin Nation. She has edited numerous publications, including *Some Posters from the NGV* (2017), *NGV Triennial* (2017), *The Centre: On Art & Urbanism in China* (2019), and *She Persists: Perspectives on Women in Art & Design* (2020). Her curatorial projects span publishing and graphic design, and include major exhibitions of the work of Experimental Jetset and Metahaven. She is a PhD candidate in the School of Architecture and Urban Design at RMIT University.

Adam Pendleton
is a New York-based artist known for work animated by what he calls "Black Dada," a critical articulation of blackness, abstraction, and the avant-garde. Pendleton makes conceptually rigorous and formally inventive paintings, collages, installations, and videos that insert his work into broader conversations about history and contemporary culture.

Simon Reynolds
is the author of eight books, including *Retromania*, the post-punk chronicle *Rip It Up and Start Again*, the rave culture history *Energy Flash*, and the glam rock study *Shock and Awe*. Born in London, currently resident in

Los Angeles, he contributes to *The Guardian*, *Pitchfork*, *The Wire*, and other magazines, and operates Blissblog (blissout.blogspot.com).

Ian F. Svenonius
is a singer, author, and talk show host based in Los Angeles. Bands include Nation of Ulysses, The Make-Up, Chain & The Gang, and Escape-ism, while books include *The Psychic Soviet* (2006), *Supernatural Strategies for Making a Rock 'n' Group* (2013), and *Censorship Now!* (2015).

McKenzie Wark
is the author of *A Hacker Manifesto*, *Gamer Theory*, *50 Years of Recuperation of the Situationist International*, and *The Beach Beneath the Street*, among other books. She teaches at the New School for Social Research and Eugene Lang College in New York City.

Lori Waxman
has been the *Chicago Tribune*'s art critic for the past decade. She performs occasionally as the "60 wrd/min art critic" and is the author of *Keep Walking Intently* (Sternberg Press, 2017), a book about the history of walking as an art form.

Mimi Zeiger
is a Los Angeles-based critic and curator.

Acknowledgements

Experimental Jetset – Superstructure
RMIT University in collaboration with NGV
Melbourne VIC, Australia
March 16 – May 5, 2018

www.experimentaljetset.nl/archive/superstructure

National Gallery of Victoria / Melbourne Design Week
Megan Patty

RMIT
Gavin Bell,
Ian Bunyi,
Layla Cluer,
Lule Garrett,
Brad Haylock,
Robert Jordan,
Síofra Lyons,
Simon Maisch,
Timothy McLeod,
Erik North,
Luke Pringipas,
Kate Rhodes,
Nella Themelios,
Tobias Titz,
Fleur Watson,
Jessica Wood

Structure & Counter-Structure
15-channel projection by Experimental Jetset, 2018

All items designed, scanned and animated by Experimental Jetset. Produced as part of *Experimental Jetset – Superstructure* at RMIT University, Melbourne

Alphabet Reform
8-channel soundtrack composed by Escape-ism (Ian F. Svenonius), 2018

Workshop voices:
Alexandra Cabral,
Ariana Papademetropoulos,
Zumi Rosow

Acknowledgements

Superstructures – Notes on Experimental Jetset / Vol. 2
Roma Publications
Amsterdam, the Netherlands
November 27, 2020

Contributors
Vasyl Cherepanyn,
Leontine Coelewij,
Linda van Deursen,
Experimental Jetset,
Owen Hatherley,
Brad Haylock,
Dirk van den Heuvel,
Lieven Lahaye,
Samata Masato,
Tom McDonough,
Kateryna Mishchenko,
Other Forms,
Mark Owens,
Megan Patty,
Adam Pendleton,
Simon Reynolds,
Ian F. Svenonius,
McKenzie Wark,
Lori Waxman,
Mimi Zeiger

Archives:

Fotomuseum, Rotterdam
collectie.nederlands
fotomuseum.nl

International Institute of Social History, Amsterdam
www.iisg.amsterdam/en

National Archive, The Hague
www.nationaalarchief.nl/en/
research

Spaarnestad Photo
www.spaarnestadphoto.nl

Stadsarchief, Amsterdam
archief.amsterdam/beeldbank

2020
2021

We like to thank our printer, publisher, contributors, friends, and family.

Postscript

rock 'n' roll nozems,
beatles and provos
have stirred the cities
on an enormous scale.
dada, cobra and
action painting
revive in the streets.

– Willem Sandberg

from: *Nu 2*,
Steendrukkerij De Jong, 1968